ECONOMIC ISSUES, PROBLEMS AND PERSPECTIVES

FISCAL EXPOSURES

SELECTED RISKS FACING THE FEDERAL BUDGET

ECONOMIC ISSUES, PROBLEMS AND PERSPECTIVES

Additional books in this series can be found on Nova's website under the Series tab.

Additional e-books in this series can be found on Nova's website under the e-book tab.

ECONOMIC ISSUES, PROBLEMS AND PERSPECTIVES

FISCAL EXPOSURES

SELECTED RISKS FACING THE FEDERAL BUDGET

LANDON P. MERRILL
EDITOR

nova publishers
New York

Library of Congress Cataloging-in-Publication Data

ISBN: 978-1-63463-589-9

Published by Nova Science Publishers, Inc. † New York

CONTENTS

PREFACE

Fiscal exposures may be explicit in that the federal government is legally required to pay for the commitment; alternatively, it may be implicit in that the exposure arises from expectations based on current policy or past practices. The federal government's long-term fiscal imbalances are driven on the spending side by the effects of an aging population and rising health care costs on Social Security and major federal health programs. However, GAO identified a variety of other fiscal exposures—responsibilities, programs, and activities that may legally commit or create the expectation for future federal spending—that vary as to source, extent of the government's legal commitment, and magnitude. This book examines selected programs that create a fiscal exposure, including the extent and estimated magnitude of the government's legal commitment; and assesses how fiscal exposures could be better recognized in the budget.

Chapter 1 – The federal government's long-term fiscal imbalances are driven on the spending side by the effects of an aging population and rising health care costs on Social Security and major federal health programs. However, GAO identified a variety of other fiscal exposures—responsibilities, programs, and activities that may legally commit or create the expectation for future federal spending—that vary as to source, extent of the government's legal commitment, and magnitude. A more complete understanding of these other fiscal exposures can help policymakers anticipate changes in future spending and enhance control and oversight over federal resources. GAO was asked to provide information on risks facing the federal budget. This report (1) examines selected programs that create a fiscal exposure, including the extent and estimated magnitude of the government's legal commitment; and (2) assesses how fiscal exposures could be better recognized in the budget. Based on its review of budget and financial data, GAO selected nine programs, including federal employee benefit programs, insurance programs, and the stock purchase agreements with Fannie Mae and Freddie Mac, and drew upon previous work to discuss potential approaches for improving budgetary attention to fiscal exposures.

Chapter 2 – Certain types of extreme weather events have become more frequent or intense according to the United States Global Change Research Program, including prolonged periods of heat, heavy downpours, and, in some regions, floods and droughts. While it is not possible to link any individual weather event to climate change, the impacts of these events affect many sectors of our economy, including the budgets of federal, state, and local governments. GAO focuses particular attention on government operations it identifies as posing a "high risk" to the American taxpayer and, in February 2013, added to its High Risk List the area *Limiting the Federal Government's Fiscal Exposure by Better Managing Climate Change Risks*. GAO's past work has identified a variety of fiscal exposures—responsibilities, programs, and activities that may explicitly or implicitly expose the federal government to future spending. This testimony is based on reports GAO issued from August 2007 to May 2014, and discusses (1) federal fiscal exposures resulting from climate-related and extreme weather impacts on critical infrastructure and federal lands, and (2) how improved federal technical assistance to all levels of government can help reduce climate-related fiscal exposures. GAO is not making new recommendations but has made numerous recommendations in prior reports on this topic, which are in varying states of implementation by the Executive Office of the President and federal agencies.

Chapter 3 – Multiple factors including increased disaster declarations, climate change effects, and insufficient premiums under the National Flood Insurance Program increase federal fiscal exposure to severe weather events. Managing fiscal exposure from climate change and the National Flood Insurance Program are both on GAO's High Risk list. GAO has previously reported that building resilience to protect against future damage is one strategy to help limit fiscal exposure. However, in prior reports GAO also identified multiple challenges to doing so. Responsibility for actions that enhance resilience rests largely outside the federal government, so nonfederal entities also play a key role. This testimony discusses (1) resilience-building challenges GAO has previously identified; (2) federal efforts to facilitate resilience-building as part of Hurricane Sandy recovery; and (3) examples of nonfederal efforts to incentivize resilience building. This testimony is based on previous GAO reports issued from 1998 through 2014 related to hazard mitigation, climate change, flood insurance, and preliminary observations from GAO's ongoing work for this committee on federal resilience efforts related to the Sandy recovery. For the ongoing work, GAO reviewed documents such as the Hurricane Sandy Rebuilding Strategy and a 2012 National Academies study on building resilience. GAO also interviewed officials from FEMA and the Department of Housing and Urban Development (HUD).

Chapter 4 – According to the United States Global Change Research Program, the costs and impacts of weather disasters resulting from floods, drought, and other events are expected to increase in significance as previously "rare" events become more common and intense. These impacts pose financial risks to the federal government. While it is not possible to link any individual weather event to climate change, these events provide insight into the potential climate-related vulnerabilities the United States faces. GAO focuses particular attention on government operations it identifies as posing a "high risk" to the American taxpayer and, in February 2013, added to its High Risk List the area *Limiting the Federal Government's Fiscal Exposure by Better Managing Climate Change Risks*. GAO's past work identified a variety of fiscal exposures—responsibilities, programs, and activities that may either legally commit the federal government to future spending or create the expectation for future spending in response to extreme weather events. This testimony is based on reports GAO issued from March 2007 to November 2013 that address these issues. GAO is not making new recommendations but made numerous recommendations in prior reports on these topics, which are in varying states of implementation by the Executive Office of the President and relevant federal agencies.

In: Fiscal Exposures
Editor: Landon P. Merrill
ISBN: 978-1-63463-589-9

Chapter 1

FISCAL EXPOSURES: IMPROVING COST RECOGNITION IN THE FEDERAL BUDGET*

United States Government Accountability Office

WHY GAO DID THIS STUDY

The federal government's long-term fiscal imbalances are driven on the spending side by the effects of an aging population and rising health care costs on Social Security and major federal health programs. However, GAO identified a variety of other fiscal exposures—responsibilities, programs, and activities that may legally commit or create the expectation for future federal spending—that vary as to source, extent of the government's legal commitment, and magnitude. A more complete understanding of these other fiscal exposures can help policymakers anticipate changes in future spending and enhance control and oversight over federal resources.

GAO was asked to provide information on risks facing the federal budget. This report (1) examines selected programs that create a fiscal exposure, including the extent and estimated magnitude of the government's legal commitment; and (2) assesses how fiscal exposures could be better recognized in the budget. Based on its review of budget and financial data, GAO selected nine programs, including federal employee benefit programs, insurance programs, and the stock purchase agreements with Fannie Mae and Freddie

* This is an edited, reformatted and augmented version of a United States Government Accountability Office publication, No. GAO-14-28, dated October 2013.

Mac, and drew upon previous work to discuss potential approaches for improving budgetary attention to fiscal exposures.

What GAO Recommends

GAO is not making new recommendations but this analysis provides additional support for past recommendations to improve budget recognition of fiscal exposures by, for example, expanding the availability and use of information on expected future spending arising from commitments made today.

What GAO Found

Fiscal exposures may be explicit in that the federal government is legally required to pay for the commitment; alternatively, it may be implicit in that the exposure arises from expectations based on current policy or past practices. The nine programs GAO examined illustrate the range of federal fiscal exposures and how they can change over time. Also, some programs may have elements of both explicit and implicit exposure. Federal insurance programs, for example, fall across the spectrum: if an event occurs, some payment is legally required—an explicit exposure. However, there may be an expectation that the government will provide assistance beyond the amount legally required—that is an implicit exposure. Prior to 2008, securities issued by Fannie Mae or Freddie Mac were explicitly not backed by the U.S. government. However, in response to the financial crisis, the government's agreement to provide temporary assistance to cover their losses up to a set amount created a new explicit exposure. The amount of future spending arising from federal fiscal exposures varies in the degree to which it is known and can be measured.

For some exposures GAO found that the budget provided incomplete information or potentially misleading signals regarding the full cost of the commitments made today. A uniform across-the-board approach to make fiscal exposures more apparent when making budget decisions may not be appropriate given their varying characteristics. Several factors need to be taken into account in selecting an approach to better recognize fiscal exposures in the budget: the extent of the government's legal commitment; the length of time until the resulting payment is made; and the extent to which the magnitude of the exposure can be reasonably estimated. Expanding the availability and use of supplemental information, including measures that can signal significant changes in the magnitude of fiscal exposures, would be an important first step to enhancing oversight over federal resources and can aid in monitoring the financial condition of programs over the longer term. Incorporating measures of the full cost into primary budget data would provide enhanced control over future spending, which can help both improve the nation's fiscal condition and enhance budgetary flexibility.

ABBREVIATIONS

CBO	Congressional Budget Office
CSRDF	Civil Service Retirement and Disability Fund
CSRS	Civil Service Retirement System
DOD	Department of Defense
DHS	Department of Homeland Security
FCIC	Federal Crop Insurance Corporation
FEHB	Federal Employee Health Benefits
FEMA	Federal Emergency Management Agency
FERS	Federal Employee Retirement System
FHFA	Federal Housing Finance Agency
Financial	*Financial Report of the United States Government Report*
GSEs	government-sponsored enterprises
MERHCF	Medicare-Eligible Retiree Health Care Fund
NDAA	National Defense Authorization Act
NFIP	National Flood Insurance Program
OMB	Office of Management and Budget
OPM	Office of Personnel Management
PBGC	Pension Benefit Guaranty Corporation
RMA	Risk Management Agency
TFL	TRICARE for Life
Treasury	Department of the Treasury
TSP	Thrift Savings Plan
VA	Department of Veterans Affairs

October 29, 2013

The Honorable Paul D. Ryan
Chairman,
Committee on the Budget
House of Representatives

Dear Mr. Chairman,

Our simulations of the federal government's long-term fiscal outlook lead to an overarching conclusion: current fiscal policy is unsustainable over the long term. In these simulations debt held by the public continues to grow over the coming decades as a share of gross domestic product. This growth is driven by a fundamental imbalance between revenue and spending, which on the spending side, is driven by the aging of the population and rising health care costs. Absent reform of federal retirement and health programs—including Social Security, Medicare, and Medicaid—federal budgetary flexibility will become increasingly constrained. In recent years, emerging issues and unanticipated events have increased awareness of additional pressures on current and future federal budgets; addressing the federal government's fiscal sustainability challenges is important for maintaining the budget flexibility to respond quickly and adequately to them. As we have reported before, understanding the longer-term budget implications of policy decisions at the time decisions are made permits more informed discussion of both overall program and specific design features. Addressing the fiscal challenges of the future will require looking at the entire range of federal activities and making difficult choices in setting priorities and linking resources to results. Consideration of the tradeoffs inherent in these decisions can be facilitated if there is comparable information on both the near-term and long-term budget implications of existing programs.

Our past work identified a variety of fiscal exposures—responsibilities, programs, and activities that may either legally commit[1] the federal government to future spending or create the expectation for future spending.[2] Fiscal exposures vary widely as to source, extent of the government's legal commitment, and magnitude. Further, some of these factors may change over time. For example, the government's response to an event or series of events can strengthen expectations that the government will respond in the same way to similar events in the future. The magnitude of the exposure in a given area may also change: for example, increased population density in coastal areas may increase the magnitude of exposures from natural disasters. A more complete understanding of the sources of fiscal exposures and the way they are changing can provide enhanced control and oversight over federal resources. Policymakers can then respond to any changing risks as they deem it appropriate.

You asked that we provide information on identifying, monitoring, and measuring new or evolving risks facing the federal budget. In this report, we (1) describe selected programs that create a fiscal exposure, including the extent and estimated magnitude of the government's legal commitment, and discuss the implications of these fiscal exposures for the budget,[3] and (2) assess how fiscal exposures could be better recognized during the budget process. Many activities can be thought of as fiscal exposures. This report focuses on a subset of fiscal exposures that represent legal commitments for future spending. We do not discuss the major social insurance programs (Social Security, Medicare, and Medicaid) and other exposures, such as disaster assistance to state and local governments or the costs of maintaining federal infrastructure, where future spending stems all or in part from implied commitments embedded in current policies or past practices.

To identify programs for our analysis, we reviewed budget and financial data from 2001 to 2012 and past work on fiscal exposures. We identified a number of programs for in-depth review that legally require the government to make payments in the future, including those where payments may be contingent on the occurrence or nonoccurrence of a given event. From that group, we selected programs in which the cost reported in the *Financial Report of the United States Government (Financial Report)* was typically greater than the amount reflected in the budget.[4] In addition, to facilitate an assessment of current budget treatment, we selected programs for which the outlays and dedicated receipts could be easily identified in budget accounts.

The fiscal exposures we discuss in this report are:

- federal crop insurance;
- national flood insurance;
- pension insurance;
- stock purchase agreements with Fannie Mae and Freddie Mac;
- civilian pension benefits;
- civilian post-retirement health benefits;
- military pension benefits;
- military post-retirement health benefits; and
- veterans compensation.

For each of these programs, we examined the extent of the government's legal commitment and estimated magnitude of the exposure by reviewing the budget, the *Financial Report*, agency documents and financial reports, and our related reports. For the federal crop insurance program, we compared outlays with resources available to the program for fiscal years 2001 to 2012. For the National Flood Insurance Program (NFIP) administered by the Federal Emergency Management Agency (FEMA) and pension insurance administered by the Pension Benefit Guaranty Corporation (PBGC), we compared the cash flows recorded in the budget account with reported changes in the net position (the difference between the program's assets and liabilities) for fiscal year 2001 to 2012. For Fannie Mae and Freddie Mac, we compared the outlays from the Department of the Treasury (Treasury) to these government-sponsored enterprises (GSEs)—as directed under the terms of the stock purchase agreements—with estimates of the government's likely commitment, as reported in the *Financial Report* for fiscal year 2008 to 2012. For federal employee benefit programs, we compared past spending and revenue data by budget account in the President's budget with estimates of costs incurred based upon the liabilities and expenses reported in the *Financial Report* or agency financial reports from fiscal years 2001 to 2012, when available.[5] For programs funded by a trust fund, we compared trust fund balances reported in the budget to estimates of the net present value of future benefits for the program, as measured by its liability in the *Financial Report*.[6] To analyze the current budget treatment of the exposures and how the budget recognition could be improved, we drew upon our body of work on fiscal exposures, including work on federal insurance and environmental disposal liabilities,[7] other nations' use of accrual budgeting to better recognize the full cost of government programs and activities,[8] and on the budget process and mechanisms to control spending and manage fiscal exposures.[9] While changes to the budget reporting may suggest the need for policy changes, our focus is on providing better information to make policy choices, not on what those choices should be.

We determined that the data from the budget were sufficiently reliable for representing the costs recognized in the budget. In our audit of the *Financial Report*, we were unable to determine the reliability of significant portions of the government's assets, liabilities, and costs, including the reliability of estimates reported for the military postretirement health benefit liability used in this report. However, we determined the data from the *Financial Report* were sufficiently reliable for representing the estimated magnitude of future spending arising from commitments incurred today. To assess the reliability of the data collected from agency financial reports for pension insurance and civilian pension liabilities, we reviewed the independent audit reports on PBGC and Office of Personnel Management's (OPM) financial statements; the auditors determined that financial information was fairly presented and therefore we determined that the data were sufficiently reliable for illustrating the programs' financial conditions.

We conducted this performance audit from September 2012 to October 2013 in accordance with generally accepted government auditing standards. Those standards require that we plan and perform the audit to obtain sufficient, appropriate evidence to provide a reasonable basis for our findings and conclusions based on our audit objectives. We believe that the evidence obtained provides a reasonable basis for our findings and conclusions based on our audit objectives.

BACKGROUND

We developed the conceptual framework for fiscal exposures in 2003, in order to facilitate the discussion of long-term costs and uncertainties that present risks for the federal budget in the future.[10] Fiscal exposures vary widely as to source, extent of the government's legal commitment, and magnitude. Figure 1 illustrates the range of the legal commitment. Fiscal exposures may be explicit in that the government is legally required to fund the commitment, or implicit in that an exposure arises not from a legal commitment, but from current policy, past practices, or other factors that may create the expectation for future spending. Some exposures present elements of both explicit and implicit exposures. Insurance programs are a key example. If an event occurs, some payment is legally required; this represents an explicit exposure. There may be an expectation that the government will provide assistance beyond the program's total available resources or budget authority (e.g., flood insurance payments made in response to a major disaster): this expectation represents an implicit exposure.

The amount of future spending arising from these exposures varies in the degree to which it is known and can be measured. For example, federal employee pension benefit payments can be reasonably estimated; accrued liabilities for earned benefits that will be paid in the future are reflected in the *Financial Report*. However, future payments to cover insured losses for events, such as terrorist attacks or catastrophic weather-related events, are more difficult to estimate due to uncertainty over whether the events will occur, when they will occur, and their severity. Estimates for some programs are further complicated when past experience indicates significant variability in payments.

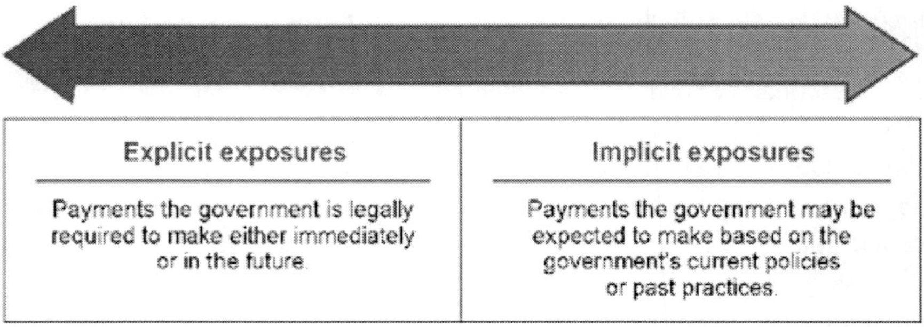

Source: GAO.

Figure 1. Spectrum of Fiscal Exposures.

Some of the largest fiscal exposures facing the federal government are the future payments for social insurance and health programs, particularly Social Security, Medicare, and the federal portion of Medicaid, which largely stem from the expectation that commitments embedded in current policies will continue.[11] Spending for these programs is expected to grow considerably in the future due to the nation's aging population and rising health care costs. Our April 2013 simulations show that spending on these programs will increase under a range of assumptions. For example, assuming current law is generally continued, spending would increase from 10 percent of GDP in 2010 to 13.6 percent of GDP by 2030, absorbing an increasing share of federal revenue and reducing future budget flexibility.[12] Should the amounts of funding needed to cover future benefits exceed the amounts available in corresponding trust funds, there may be an expectation that the government will use federal funds to pay the difference, even though there would be no legal commitment on behalf of the government to do so. Significant information on the estimated future spending for Social Security and Medicare is available; in addition to our long-term fiscal simulations, the Congressional Budget Office (CBO) and the administration regularly publish long-term fiscal simulations, which illustrate the expected growth in spending for these programs.[13]

Future spending for other implicit exposures can be more difficult to estimate. For example, the frequency and magnitude of declared disasters has increased in recent decades, resulting in billions of dollars of supplemental appropriations. FEMA has obligated over $80 billion in federal assistance for disasters declared during fiscal year 2004 through 2011. The unpredictable nature of such events makes estimating future spending difficult.

In some instances, current budget treatment does not fully capture or facilitate explicit consideration of some fiscal exposures at the time policy or program design decisions are made because some primary budget data—receipts and outlays—are generally measured on a cash or cash-equivalent basis—that is, when cash is received or paid, rather than when costs are incurred. For programs where the time between the incurrence of a cost and resulting payment is relatively short, the budget often provides sufficient information on and control over the government's spending commitments. However, for some programs, where cash flows to and from the government span many budget periods, or where the government legally obligates itself to make future payments or incur losses if an event occurs in the future, the generally cash-based measures used in the budget do not reflect the magnitude of the government's legal commitment of future resources at the time decisions are being made. If the full cost of a spending decision is included in the budget when the decision is made, then decision makers can consider the total costs when setting priorities, comparing the cost of a program with its benefits, or assessing the cost of one method of reaching a specified goal with another. Decision makers' ability to make informed choices would be improved by increased transparency regarding the impact of policy decisions on the expected path of spending and revenue. Expected future spending arising from some exposures is recognized in the financial statements, which report costs on an accrual basis. Generally, under financial accounting standards, liabilities are recorded for probable and measureable outflows of resources arising from past transactions and events. Also, under accounting standards, the cost of claims for federal insurance programs that are deemed probable and measurable is considered a liability; reasonably possible losses are disclosed in the notes to the financial statements. Therefore, some measures reported in the government's financial statements can be useful indicators of future spending arising from certain fiscal exposures.

THE BUDGET PROVIDES INCOMPLETE INFORMATION ABOUT SOME FISCAL EXPOSURES

The nine programs we examined illustrate a range of fiscal exposures in which the extent of the government's legal commitment varies (see figure 2).[14]

For example, civilian pension benefits are explicit exposures because the government has a legal commitment to pay pension benefits earned by current employees who will receive benefits in the future and to pay retirees who currently receive benefits. Other fiscal exposures, such as federal insurance programs, fall across the spectrum. For example, if extreme weather causes crop losses, the government is legally required to provide funds to cover associated crop insurance claims. However, there are some insurance programs—such as pension insurance—for which the government is not legally required to cover claim losses in excess of available resources. Pension insurance claims up to the statutory limit are explicit exposures; losses in excess of PBGC's available resources represent an implicit exposure for the federal government to the extent there is an expectation that the government would step in and cover losses beyond the program's reserves.[15]

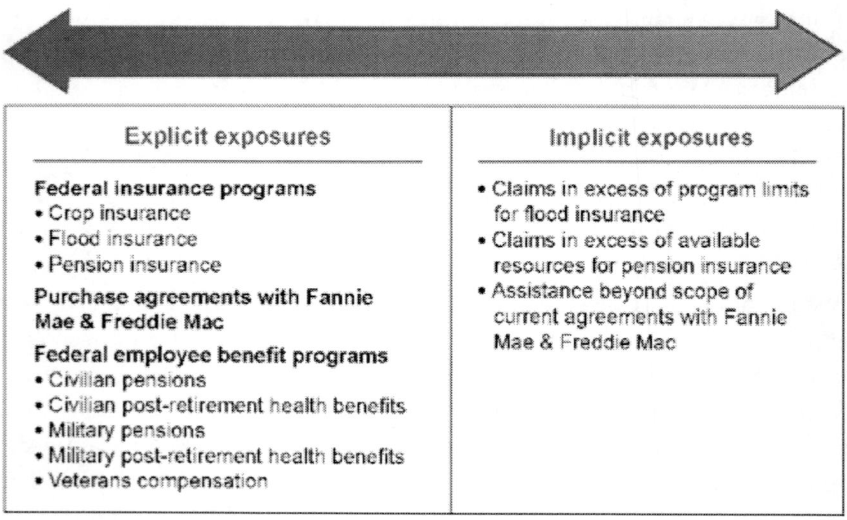

Source: GAO.

Figure 2. Selected Programs Illustrate Range of Fiscal Exposures.

For some exposures, the extent of the government's legal commitment has changed over time. For example, the fiscal exposure created by Fannie Mae and Freddie Mac changed in recent years as the government responded to the financial crisis. Prior to 2008, securities issued by Fannie Mae and Freddie Mac were explicitly not guaranteed by the federal government and the government had no legal responsibility to provide support to these GSEs. However, in response to the financial crisis, the government placed them into conservatorship and agreed to provide temporary assistance, creating a new explicit exposure.[16]

The budget does reflect some or all of the cost of the government's legal commitment for some exposures. For example, for crop insurance, budget authority[17] is provided to cover the cost of premium subsidies, claims payments, and administrative expense subsidies. For military and civilian pensions, agencies are required to make contributions out of current budget authority to cover some of the costs of civilian and military pension benefits earned by current employees. These contributions reduce the funds available to each agency to fund other activities. However, the recognition is incomplete because the contributions are not set to cover the full cost. In addition, we found that the budget provides incomplete information or potentially misleading signals about today's legal commitments for some other exposures as well. Our selected fiscal exposures generally demonstrate one or more of the following characteristics:

The full cost of commitments incurred today is not recorded in the budget until the corresponding outlays are made in the future. For example, for veterans compensation and civilian post-retirement health benefits, the budget reflects benefit payments in a given year, instead of capturing the cost of benefits earned today that will need to be paid in the future.

Similarly, the cost of pension insurance accrued in a given year is not reflected in the budget; rather, premiums are shown as receipts when they are collected and payments are shown as outlays when they are made. This focus on annual cash flows does not reflect the government's cost for pension insurance because the time between the extension of the insurance, the receipt of premiums and other collections, the occurrence of an insured event, and the payment of claims may extend over several decades. Rather, the cost of pension insurance can be measured by the portion of risk assumed by the government that is not charged to the beneficiary—a "missing premium."[18] This subsidy is not recognized in the budget when the insurance is extended.

The current budget treatment results in both incomplete information with regard to any missing premium, and in potentially misleading information about the program's financial condition. For example, at the time budget decisions were being made for fiscal year 2013, the budget showed a positive budget estimate (i.e., net revenues) for PBGC of about $1.6 billion, suggesting that the program would help decrease the federal budget deficit that year. However, the financial reports available at the same time showed the program's net position worsened by about $8 billion from the year before, principally as the result of incurred losses that are not yet reflected in the budget. These estimates provide significantly different pictures of the program's health and its potential draw on future budget resources. While PBGC can legally only pay claims up to the amount of resources available in its revolving funds, in the face of major pension fund failures there might be an expectation that the government would pass legislation allowing PBGC to cover some or all of the gap.[19]

Dedicated resources are estimated to be insufficient to pay for the associated commitment. Some programs set aside amounts out of current budget authority to cover benefits earned today but payable in the future. For example, agency contributions and Treasury payments to cover military pension benefits accrued during the year are deposited in a budgetary trust fund; however, the trust fund balance is significantly less than expected future benefits payments, as measured by the accrued liability (see appendix I, figure 9). As such, the trust fund's balance can provide a signaling function of future spending but does not necessarily represent the full cost of those legal commitments.[20]

Furthermore, some insurance programs do not have sufficient dedicated resources to cover expected costs. For example, the NFIP historically insured many properties at a subsidized rate.[21] In addition, overall flood insurance premiums were designed to permit the program to cover losses and expenses in an "average historical loss year," but not to cover high-loss years. Instead, the program was given the authority to borrow from the Treasury in such years, with the expectation that low-loss years would allow the program to repay any borrowed funds. With the exception of years involving catastrophes, annual losses and receipts have generally evened out since 1978, but NFIP has been unable to repay the amounts borrowed in response to catastrophic events, such as Hurricane Katrina in 2005. This funding structure is one of the reasons the program was added to our High Risk List in 2006.[22]

Increasing amounts of future spending may be required or expected based both on recent trends and events—and on the government's response to those events. For example, weather-related events have cost the nation tens of billions of dollars in damages over the past decade. The exposure from weather-related events increases with changes in population density as well as increased frequency and severity of the events. This is one reason we added the federal government's fiscal exposure created by climate change to our 2013 High Risk List.[23] Through federal programs like flood and crop insurance, these events pose significant financial risks for the federal government.

Approaches to Better Recognize the Programs that Create Fiscal Exposures in the Budget

Given the variation in fiscal exposures, when making budget decisions, a uniform, across-the-board approach to make fiscal exposures more apparent may not be appropriate. Several factors need to be taken into account in selecting an approach to better recognize fiscal exposures in the budget: the extent of the government's legal commitment; the length of time until the resulting payment is made; and the extent to which the magnitude of the exposure can be reasonably estimated. We previously recommended to OMB and Congress two general approaches: reporting supplemental information in budget documents to increase attention to fiscal exposures, and incorporating costs into primary budget data to allow for better comparisons among programs.

Reporting Supplemental Information Can Increase Attention to Fiscal Exposures

Supplemental reporting involves including information about the financial state of programs in addition to that which is available in primary budget data. Improved supplemental reporting in budget documents on fiscal exposures would make information more accessible to policymakers without introducing additional complexity and uncertainty directly into the budget. With a supplemental reporting approach, the current basis of reporting primary budget data would not be changed. Instead, the supplemental information would be used along with budget data to identify important signals that could be used to monitor fiscal exposures. For example, the Appendix Volume in the President's budget includes a balance sheet for some federal insurance programs that shows the program's net position (assets minus liabilities), providing valuable information about the program's affect on future budget resources. For the Federal Crop Insurance budget account, a supplemental table includes the cost of the premium subsidy provided by the government. In 2003, we recommended that OMB create an annual report on fiscal exposures providing a concise list and description of such exposures, cost estimates (where possible), and an assessment of methodologies and data used to produce cost estimates for such exposures. We further recommended that OMB report estimated costs of certain exposures as a new budget concept—"exposure level"—as a notational item in the Program and Financing schedule of the President's budget, though the recommendation was not implemented.

In some cases, improving supplemental reporting in key budget documents may simply be a matter of expanding program analysis and making existing analytical work more readily available. For example, CBO regularly prepares 10-year budget projections for several programs in our review. While this time period is helpful for many programs, longer-term projections would be helpful for those programs—such as federal employee pensions and retiree health—where the time between the legal commitment and payments can extend over several decades. Further, significant changes in expected spending (or differences between actual and estimated spending) should prompt analysis, including consideration of the nature and source of the change.

Identifying meaningful measures that would provide signals about the changing nature or magnitude of the exposure might offer another means to focus policymaker attention on fiscal exposures. For example, trust fund balances can serve as a signaling function for decision makers about underlying fiscal imbalances in covered programs.[24] A gap between the projected fund balance and expected spending can signal that the fund, either by design or because of changes in circumstances, is collecting insufficient monies to finance future payments. Also, the repeated use of borrowing authority[25] could be an indicator that the magnitude of the exposure has changed. Specifically, NFIP was expected to borrow in "above-average claim" years and repay that borrowing in "below-average claim" years. In years with extraordinarily high claims resulting from catastrophes like Superstorm Sandy and Hurricane Katrina, NFIP has used the borrowing authority repeatedly. The program currently has an outstanding debt to the Treasury of $24 billion. The program's inability to cover claims in excess of premiums led to the passage of legislation in 2012 that altered the design of the program, including a key provision that NFIP raise premium rates to reflect true flood risk and make the program more financially stable.[26] These signaling devices can provide policymakers with information regarding the full costs involved in budget decisions and enable those concerned about exposures to raise questions and challenges in the budget debate and to prompt action.

Incorporating the Full Costs of Legal Commitments Incurred Today into Primary Budget Data Would Allow for Better Comparisons among Programs

A second potential approach to improving recognition of fiscal exposures is incorporating full costs into primary budget data. This method would allow for better comparisons among competing priorities and between different methods for achieving program goals. In certain cases, including credit programs and government employee pensions, accrual accounting methods are already used to some extent in budgeting. For example, credit reform in 1990 permitted more accurate comparisons among direct loans, loan guarantees, and other types of tools for achieving a program's objectives. Some other countries, such as Canada and Iceland, also use accrual budgeting selectively to increase recognition of future cash requirements related to service provided during the year; officials from these countries generally said that accrual budgeting contributed to improved resource allocation and program management decisions in these specific areas. We have recommended that Congress expand the use of accrual budgeting to other budget program areas where it would enhance upfront control, such as insurance and environmental liabilities.[27] While it has not been expanded to these areas, proposals addressing broader budget process reform have included accrual budgeting. As seen in the implementation of credit reform, including estimates of full costs in primary data may also lead to the development of better estimates of future spending, though it would require the development of methodologies appropriate to the nature of the exposure.

Because the cost to the government varies according to the specific program's design and characteristics, different types of cost estimates could be incorporated into primary budget data in order to better recognize the government's fiscal exposure. For example,

- **Normal cost:** For retirement benefit programs, such as pension or retiree health, the normal cost is the actuarial present value of the benefits to be paid in the future that are attributable to employees' current year of service. As such, it is one measure of an accrual cost for a particular year.
- **Risk-assumed cost estimates:**[28] For insurance programs, key information is whether premiums will be sufficient to pay for covered losses under existing policies. The portion of risk assumed by the government that is not charged to the beneficiary—the "missing

premium" or subsidy cost—is essentially the difference between some measure of the full premium and the actual premium charged to the insured. This cost measure has been used since 1991 for credit programs.

All estimates of future spending introduce some degree of additional uncertainty into the budget and the ease of implementation differs. Some measures may already be used widely in other forms of reporting, whereas others are relatively new concepts for federal budget reporting and may involve developing new models and technical skills. Despite any implementation challenges, approximate estimates of the full cost to government may be preferable to some current measures that are incomplete or potentially misleading. Further, a requirement to produce estimates for budget reporting may help improve the quality of estimates by drawing more attention to them. Although using estimates may introduce uncertainty in primary budget data, it would result in earlier cost recognition in the budget. This would help reinforce up-front controls in the budget process.

Concluding Observations

Over the past decade, the magnitude of some fiscal exposures has grown and the extent of the government's commitment for some exposures has changed due to events and trends and the government's response to them. These fiscal exposures will require future federal spending and will absorb resources available for other activities. The federal budget both allocates and controls resources, but does not provide complete information about some significant fiscal exposures. Therefore, we continue to support many past recommendations to improve budget recognition of these fiscal exposures, both to increase the attention given to them and also to allow for more comparable cost information for decision makers to consider when determining the best way to achieve various policy goals or to design a program. Expanding the availability and use of supplemental information—including measures that can signal the significant changes in the magnitude and nature of fiscal exposures facing the federal government—would be an important first step toward enhancing control and oversight over federal resources and can aid in monitoring the financial condition of programs over the longer term. Incorporating measures of the full cost into primary budget data would provide enhanced control over future spending. This can both improve the nation's fiscal condition and enhance the budgetary flexibility for responding to unexpected or emerging challenges.

AGENCY COMMENTS AND OUR EVALUATION

We provided a draft of this report to the Office of Management and Budget and the agencies responsible for administering the programs we reviewed. Those agencies are the Risk Management Agency (RMA) in the Department of Agriculture; the Federal Housing and Finance Administration; Department of Defense (DOD); Department of Homeland Security (DHS); Department of Veterans Affairs (VA); the Office of Personnel Management; and the Pension Benefit Guaranty Corporation (PBGC). RMA, DOD, PBGC, and the Federal Emergency Management Agency in DHS provided technical comments that were incorporated in the report as appropriate.

VA generally agreed with our findings and stated that current budget reporting provides adequate information for determining the resources necessary to pay benefits for current veterans and survivors. While we agree that the budget records the outlays associated with benefits paid in a given year, we maintain that current budget reporting provides incomplete information about the costs incurred for benefits earned during the year that will be paid in the future.

Sincerely yours,
Susan J. Irving
Director for Federal Budget Analysis
Strategic Issues

APPENDIX I: INFORMATION ON SELECTED FISCAL EXPOSURES

This appendix describes the extent and estimated magnitude of the fiscal exposure created by nine programs:

- federal crop insurance;
- national flood insurance;
- pension insurance;

- stock purchase agreements with Fannie Mae and Freddie Mac;
- civilian pension benefits;
- civilian post-retirement health benefits;
- military pension benefits;
- military post-retirement health benefits; and
- veterans compensation.

Federal Crop Insurance

Background

Farming has always been vulnerable to risks from natural causes such as drought, excessive moisture, hail, wind, frost, insects, and disease. Farmers are also exposed to financial losses from price risk. The federal government helps mitigate the impact of these risks on farm income through the federal crop insurance program. Crop insurance is sold and serviced by 17 approved private companies. Under the provisions of these agreements, the private companies both bear a percentage of any loss and reap a percentage of any gain associated with the policies over the course of the year. The federal government subsidizes the premiums paid by farmers and acts as primary reinsurer for the private companies that underwrite the policies. The federal government also makes payments to insurance companies that are intended to cover administrative expenses for selling and servicing crop insurance policies. Federal crop insurance is not intended to be self-financing through premiums; a permanent, indefinite appropriation covers any payments that are needed to cover losses and other expenses.

Extent and Estimated Magnitude of the Exposure

The government's legal commitment to pay crop insurance policyholder claims when losses occur makes the program an explicit exposure. The amount of federal spending resulting from this exposure depends on the extent of losses incurred by farmers.

The federal crop insurance program's costs increased sharply in recent years. An indicator of the government's exposure is the increase in appropriations drawn from the general fund,[1] which have grown from \$3.4 billion in fiscal year 2001 to \$7.6 billion in fiscal year 2012 as shown in figure 3.

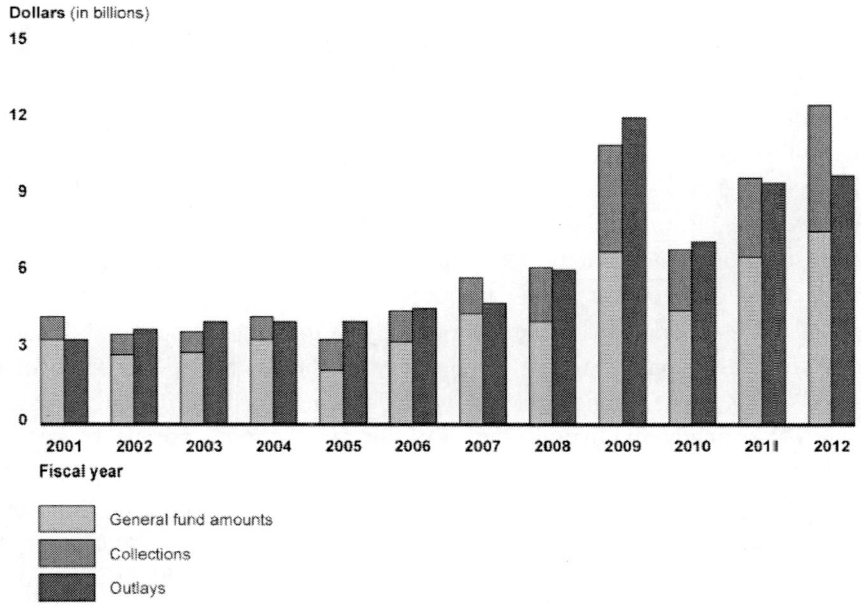

Source: GAO analysis of OMB data.

Note: Data from the President's Budget Appendix. General fund amounts, collections, and outlays from the Program and Financing Schedule. Amounts received by the Crop Insurance Corporation through the general fund are appropriated and represent premium subsidies as authorized by section 508(b) of the Federal Crop Insurance Act, as amended. Collections primarily come from premiums paid by farmers. Outlays primarily represent payments for indemnities to insured farmers and administrative expenses for approved insurance providers.

Figure 3. Federal Crop Insurance Corporation, Outlays and Resources, Fiscal Years 2001 through 2012.

Budget Treatment of the Exposure

Figure 3 shows outlays and resources available to the program, the combination of the general revenue funds, and collections (primarily premiums) received. Outlays, which reflect claims payments and other associated costs, doubled from $3 billion in 2001 to $6 billion in 2008, and then doubled again in 2009 to $12 billion. Premiums received do not fully cover the program's costs; general revenue funds make up more than half of the program's available resources and are used in part to provide premium and administrative expense subsidies. Therefore, the full cost of the crop insurance subsidies and administrative costs is reflected in the budget.

Key Factors to Consider

Anticipating the future budget exposure presented by crop insurance is complicated by the potential impact of climate change and changes in program design. Our March 2007 report assessing the financial risks to the Federal Crop Insurance Corporation (FCIC) found that its exposure to weather related losses had grown substantially. At that time, we found that little had been done to develop the kind of information needed to understand FCIC's long-term exposure to climate change and that FCIC had not analyzed the potential impacts of an increase in the frequency or the severity of weather-related events on its operations. Since then, a study examining the potential impact of climate change on the federal crop insurance program was prepared for the Risk Management Agency (RMA), which administers the program. According to RMA officials, the overall impact of climate change is not clear, given the uncertainty of various climate change scenarios and the potential adaptive responses by growers and the crop insurance program. Reflecting these uncertainties and the significance of this issue, we included a discussion of the crop insurance program in a high risk designation related to the fiscal exposure of climate change in our High Risk List in 2013.[2]

National Flood Insurance

Background

The Federal Emergency Management Agency (FEMA) within the Department of Homeland Security operates the National Flood Insurance Program (NFIP) to provide flood insurance to residential and commercial property owners. Flood insurance is funded primarily through premium collections. The premiums were designed to permit the program to cover losses and expenses in an "average historical loss year," but not to cover high-loss years. Instead, the program has statutory authority to borrow from the Treasury in such years with the expectation that low-loss years would allow the program to repay any borrowed funds. While not always the case, since 1978 annual losses have generally evened out with receipts over normal years but borrowing authority has been accessed and increased in recent years, in response to catastrophic events such as Hurricane Katrina in 2005.

Extent and Estimated Magnitude of the Exposure

NFIP presents a range of exposures to the federal government. The government's legal commitment to pay flood insurance policyholder claims when losses occur makes the program an explicit exposure. The amount of federal spending resulting from this exposure depends, in part, on the frequency of weather-related events and their severity. If total claims exceed amounts available from premium collections, NFIP may access available borrowing authority to cover excess claim amounts. To the extent there is an expectation that the federal government cover claims exceeding the amount that NFIP has been authorized to borrow from the Treasury, NFIP represents an implicit exposure. NFIP received increased borrowing authority in 2013 to cover loss claims related to Superstorm Sandy. Including the $16.8 billion NFIP borrowed to cover claims primarily from Katrina, the program's reported total outstanding debt had increased to $24 billion as of March 31, 2013.

One measure of the government's exposure is the extent to which claims exceed available resources. One indicator of the exposure is NFIP's net position—the residual difference between the program's total assets and liabilities.[3] NFIP's liabilities include outstanding debt to the Treasury. As shown in figure 4, the program's reported net position declined dramatically from fiscal year 2006 to fiscal year 2007 as NFIP borrowed from the Treasury to pay claims related to Hurricane Katrina. At the end of fiscal year 2012, the program's net position was negative $19 billion; this did not reflect the additional borrowing in 2013.

Budget Treatment of the Exposure

Figure 4 also shows how the program is reflected in primary budget data. NFIP is reflected on a cash basis: premium collections are recorded as receipts in the year they are received and claims payments are recorded as outlays in the year they are made. The balance sheet for NFIP is also included in the budget as supplementary information. However, the budget has not reflected the subsidy cost—or "missing premium"— embedded in NFIP's program design. The subsidy can be measured as the portion of risk assumed by the government that is not charged to the beneficiary.

Key Factors to Consider

NFIP was first added to our High Risk List in 2006 because of concerns about financial solvency. The program was highlighted again in 2013 when we added the fiscal exposure of climate change to the High Risk List.[4] In 2007, we found that more information was needed to understand and manage the program's long-term exposure to climate change and analyze the potential effects of an increase in the frequency or in the severity of weather-related events on their operations, which in turn affects the fiscal exposure to the government. In June 2013, AECOM released a FEMA-sponsored study to investigate the potential impacts of climate change and population growth on the NFIP.[5] Recent legislation may address some of these concerns. In 2012, NFIP was required to set actuarially sound premium rates and phase out the premium subsidy on certain properties, as well as establish a reserve fund to cover catastrophic losses.[6] We have reported that the financial reforms included in the Biggert-Waters Act could go a long way toward reducing the fiscal exposure created by the program, but they will be phased in over time and it is too early to make conclusions.

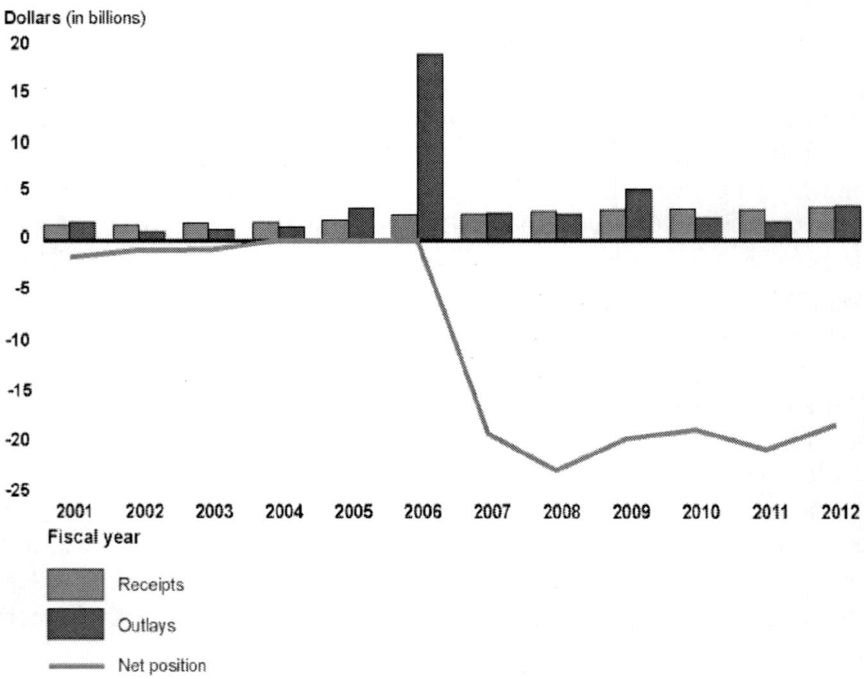

Source: GAO analysis of OMB data.

Note: Data from the President's Budget Appendix. Receipts and outlays from the Program and Financing Schedule; GAO analyzed supplemental balance sheet information on assets and liabilities to determine the net position.

Figure 4. National Flood Insurance Receipts, Outlays, and Net Position, Fiscal Years 2001 through 2012.

Pension Insurance

Background

The Pension Benefit Guaranty Corporation (PBGC) is a wholly-owned government corporation established under the Employee Retirement Income Security Act of 1974[7] to protect the pension benefits of American workers. PBGC operates two insurance programs—one for single employer plans and another for multiemployer plans, which are created by collective bargaining agreements and include more than one employer. While the single employer program is supported by both premiums and an asset base, the multiemployer program is supported mainly by premiums and a relatively small asset base. As of the end of fiscal year 2012, PBGC insured the benefits for nearly 43 million workers, retirees, and beneficiaries participating in about 26,000 private sector defined benefit pension plans. PBGC is required to be self-financing and does not receive any funds from general revenue. It funds its operations through insurance premiums paid by companies that sponsor defined benefit pension plans, investment income, and assets from terminated plans. Premiums charged are set by law. PBGC's financial activities are included in both the federal budget and consolidated financial statements of the U.S. government.

Extent and Estimated Magnitude of the Exposure

Pension insurance presents a range of exposures to the federal government. PBGC's legal commitment to pay pension benefit guarantees when losses occur makes the program an explicit exposure for the government.[8] While the federal government may not cover losses related to failed pension plans in excess of PBGC's available resources, the extent to which there is an expectation (under some circumstances) that the federal government would step in and change the law to make all or some of such payments represents an implicit exposure.[9]

One measure of the magnitude of the government's fiscal exposure is PBGC's net position, which represents the residual difference between PBGC's total assets and liabilities. As figure 5 shows, PBGC's net position generally declined from a $7.8 billion surplus in 2001 to a $34 billion deficit in fiscal year 2012. However, PBGC estimated that its financial risk for potential termination of underfunded plans sponsored by financially weak firms to be almost $300 billion. Although PBGC's annual receipts currently exceed its outlays, its overall financial position is weaker than would be indicated by these annual receipts and outlays.

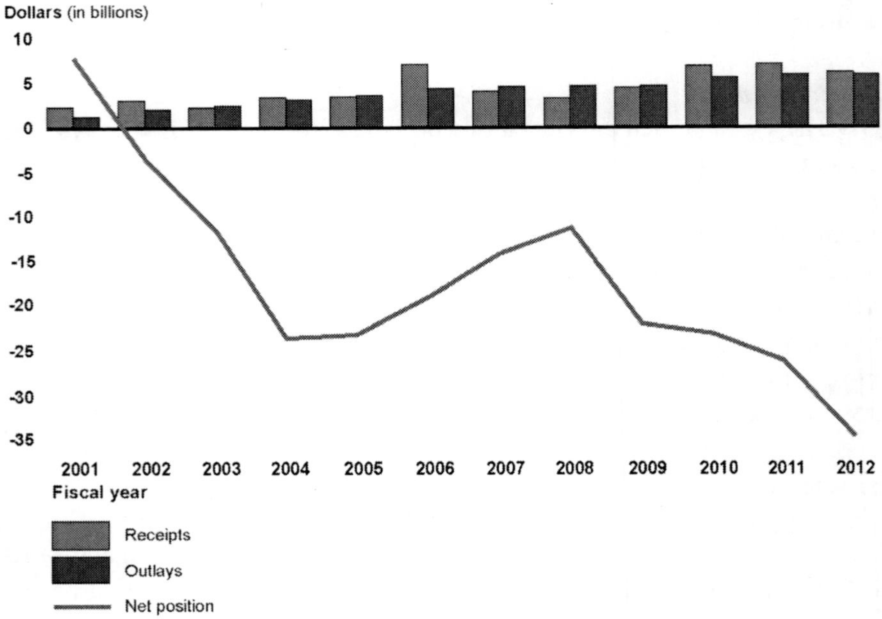

Source: GAO analysis of OMB and PBGC data.

Notes: Receipts and outlays from the President's Budget Appendix. Net position from PBGC's financial reports.

Figure 5. Pension Benefit Guaranty Corporation Net Position and Revolving Fund Cash Flows, Fiscal Years 2001 through 2012.

Budget Treatment of the Exposure

PBGC is an example of a program for which cash-based budgeting provides potentially misleading information. Premiums are shown as receipts when they come into the Treasury and payments are shown as outlays when they are made; the time lag between these events means that an increase in PBGC premiums would appear in the budget as an increase in revenues. The budget does not reflect the "missing premium"—the portion of a full risk-based premium not charged to the insured, which could be a signal of the expected cost of the program.

Key Factors to Consider

In 2013, we reported that plan terminations and insolvencies threaten PBGC's ability to pay pension guarantees for retirees. In the event that the agency were to exhaust all of its assets and become insolvent, the agency would only have premium revenue to rely on to make its benefit payments.[10]

As a consequence, PBGC would be forced to seek additional federal funding, dramatically cut benefit payments to participants, or ask Congress to raise premiums significantly to meet its benefit commitments.[11] We, along with PBGC, have expressed concerns that the current level of premiums and assets will not be sufficient to cover expected claims in the future.[12] PBGC has been on our High Risk List since 2003. Because of long-term challenges related to its governance and funding structure, PBGC's financial future is uncertain. While Congress and PBGC have taken steps in recent years to address these challenges, PBGC continues to face the risk of significant increases in liabilities and inadequate sources of revenue to finance future claims.

Stock Purchase Agreements with Fannie Mae and Freddie Mac

Background

Congress established Fannie Mae and Freddie Mac as government-sponsored enterprises (GSEs) in the housing finance market to support the supply of mortgage loans; securities issued by these GSEs were not backed by the full faith and credit of the government. In 2008, in response to the financial crisis, Treasury entered into Senior Preferred Stock Purchase Agreements (the agreements) with Fannie Mae and Freddie Mac to preserve the assets and mitigate systemic risks that contributed to market instability. Under the agreements, Treasury would purchase these GSEs' senior preferred stock and make funds available on a quarterly basis, to be recovered by redemption of the stock or by other means. While the initial funding commitment for each enterprise was capped at $100 billion, Treasury increased the cap to $200 billion per GSE in May 2009 to maintain confidence in these GSEs. In 2012, the caps were replaced with a formulaic cap allowing these GSEs to make quarterly draws based upon their net position, or if the liabilities of either GSE, individually, exceed its respective assets.

Extent and Estimated Magnitude of the Exposure

The purchase agreements with Fannie Mae and Freddie Mac illustrate how an exposure can change over time. Prior to 2008, these GSEs represented an implicit fiscal exposure to the government because the securities they issued were explicitly not guaranteed by the full faith and credit of the U.S. government. The 2008 stock purchase agreements, while temporary, created a new explicit exposure for the federal government to provide immediate financial support to Fannie Mae and Freddie Mac. At the end of any quarter in which either Fannie Mae's or Freddie Mac's balance sheet reflects that total liabilities exceed total assets, the GSEs have 15 business days to request funds under the terms of the agreements. Treasury then has 60 days to provide the funds, as necessary, up to the maximum amount of the funding commitment. The federal government is not obligated to provide additional assistance beyond the scope of the agreements, but the government's response may influence expectations related to future support. This expectation represents an implicit exposure.

One measure of the magnitude of the exposure to the government is the liability reported in the 2012 *Financial Report of the United States Government (Financial Report)* of $9 billion, reflecting Treasury's best estimate at the time of likely draws over the remaining duration of the agreements. The liability was significantly reduced in 2012 (see figure 6). This reduction was in part due to a revision to the agreements that is expected to reduce the amount of future draws, and also to the improved housing market, which contributed positively to the GSEs financial results. Another possible measure of the exposure is the remaining draw authority available to these GSEs, which was about $258 billion as of January 1, 2013. This represents the maximum amount of future spending under the current agreement. In considering the exposure under either measure, any amounts received related to the federal government's investment in the GSEs' stock—which had a reported fair value of $109.3 billion in the 2012 *Financial Report*— would reduce the federal government's exposure.

Budget Treatment of the Exposure

Figure 6 also shows the Treasury payments to these GSEs and draw authority balance at the end of the year as recorded in primary budget data. The Administration considers Fannie Mae and Freddie Mac to be outside of the budget; therefore payments to them are recorded as outlays. Since 2008, Fannie Mae and Freddie Mac have drawn a total of $187.5 billion and draws have decreased each year—from a high of $95.6 billion in fiscal year 2009 to $18.5 billion in fiscal year 2012. The draw authority balance remaining at the end of each fiscal year is reflected as an unobligated balance.

Under the terms of the agreements, the cost of the government's commitment is offset by dividend payments from these GSEs to Treasury.[13] As figure 6 shows, in fiscal year 2012 Treasury made payments to these GSEs of $18.5 billion but these GSEs made $18.4 billion in dividend payments to the Treasury. Including $14.6 billion in dividend payments due as of

September 2013, the aggregate dividend payments to Treasury from Fannie Mae and Freddie Mac totaled about $146 billion.

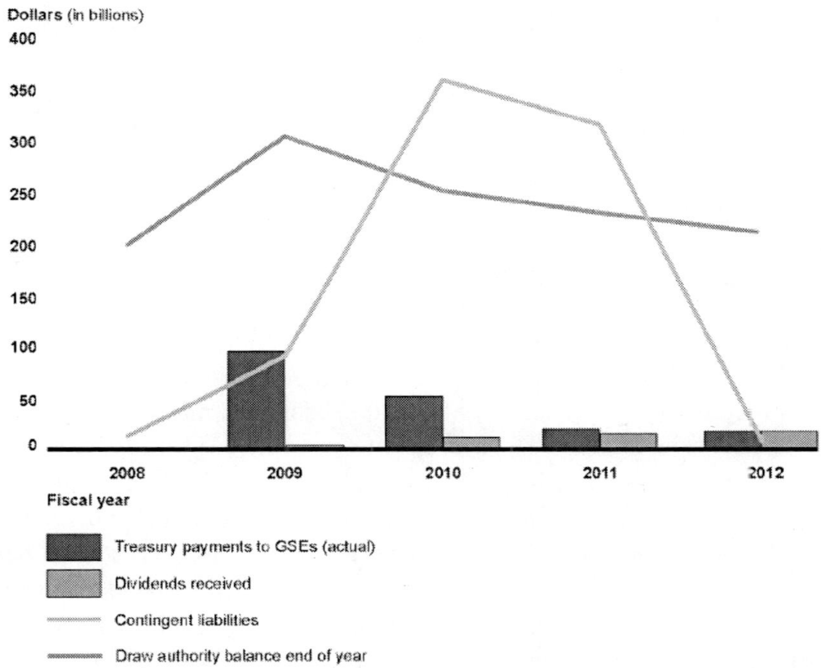

Source: GAO analysis of data from OMB, Treasury, and Fannie Mae and Freddie Mac.

Note: Treasury payments to GSEs based on data from the President's Budget Appendix. Contingent liabilities from the *Financial Reports*. Dividends and draw authority balances based on data from Fannie Mae and Freddie Mac.

Figure 6. Treasury Agreements with Fannie Mae and Freddie Mac, Fiscal Years 2008 through 2012.

Key Factors to Consider

We, federal regulators, researchers, and others have long argued that, despite the federal government explicitly not guaranteeing the enterprises' debt or including them in the federal budget, Fannie Mae and Freddie Mac had financial incentives to engage in risky business practices to strengthen their profitability in part because of the financial benefits derived from an implied federal guarantee on their financial obligations. In 2009, we reported that excluding Fannie Mae and Freddie Mac from federal budget totals leads to limited transparency about these GSEs' risks and potential costs to taxpayers.[14] This is in contrast to the budget treatment for direct federal loan and loan guarantee programs, which record associated costs in the federal budget.[15] The future structures of these two GSEs and the roles they will serve in the mortgage market must still be determined and will affect future decisions about budget treatment.

Civilian Pension Benefits

Background

Most federal civilian employees are covered by one of two pension plans, depending largely on when they began their federal service: those hired before 1984 are covered by the Civil Service Retirement System (CSRS) while most employees who entered federal service after 1983 are covered by the Federal Employee Retirement System (FERS).[16] The difference between the design and structure of these two plans affects the extent and magnitude of the fiscal exposure each presents to the government.

CSRS is a stand-alone defined benefit plan enacted in 1920.[17] CSRS employees do not pay Social Security payroll taxes and they do not earn Social Security benefits for their CSRS-covered service.[18] FERS has a small defined benefit portion—the FERS annuity—which supplements Social Security, and a voluntary defined contribution portion, the Thrift Savings Plan (TSP).[19] Defined contribution plans do not represent a fiscal exposure to the government because benefits in retirement are based on contributions and investment returns in these accounts. The analysis in this report covers CSRS and the FERS annuity—the defined benefit portion of FERS—which constitutes the government's exposure arising from the two civilian pension plans.

Both agency and employee contributions toward CSRS and the FERS defined benefit annuity are paid to the Civil Service Retirement and Disability Fund (CSRDF), the trust fund in the budget dedicated to funding civilian pension benefits. The CSRDF also receives some payments from the Treasury's general fund account (largely intended to amortize and pay interest on the previously accumulated CSRS liability) and the CSRDF is credited with interest (investment income) on the Treasury securities it holds.[20]

Extent and Estimated Magnitude of the Exposure

Civilian pension benefits are explicit exposures because the government has a legal commitment to pay pension benefits earned by current employees who will receive benefits in the future and retirees who currently receive benefits.

From a government-wide perspective, the magnitude of the exposure can be estimated by the accrued liability for defined benefit civilian pensions, which at the end of fiscal year 2012 was estimated to be $1.8 trillion, up from $1.2 trillion in 2001. Most of the accrued pension liability is the cost of CSRS and FERS benefits earned but not yet paid to date.[21] The composition of the civilian pension liability has changed and will continue to change over time because the extent and magnitude of the government's exposure are different for CSRS and FERS. This reflects both the transition from CSRS to FERS in the mid 1980s, and the differences in their benefit structure.

- Since employees hired after 1984 are covered by FERS, that liability is growing faster than the CSRS liability, which should diminish as more CSRS employees retire and the vast majority of the civilian workforce is covered by FERS.[22]
- The CSRS liability is greater largely due to the difference in size of the benefit, not the number of participants. Specifically, the cost to the government for CSRS is greater than for FERS, which provides a smaller defined benefit plan that is augmented by Social Security and the TSP.[23]
- Although agencies and employees both make contributions for CSRS, it was largely designed as a pay-as-you-go program. Agency and employee contributions were not set at a level to cover the full cost of benefits as they are earned—even with investment income.[24] CSRS employee and agency contributions are each set at 7 percent of pay for a total 14 percent contribution. However, for fiscal year 2012, the Office of Personnel Management (OPM) estimated that the amount required to fully fund future CSRS benefits—the normal cost—is 32 percent of pay.[25]
- The FERS defined benefit annuity is designed to be fully funded by employee and agency contributions and investment income. Agency contributions for FERS employees are based on annual calculations of the amount required to fully fund future benefits (normal cost) less the employee contribution rate. Employee contributions are calculated differently for FERS than for CSRS: FERS employees essentially pay the difference between the CSRS employee contribution rate of 7 percent and the Social Security employee payroll tax rate, currently 6.2 percent, for an employee contribution rate of 0.8 percent.

However, in 2012, the employee contribution was increased to 3.1 percent of pay for employees hired after December 31, 2012, effectively reducing the agency contribution.[26]

The transition from CSRS to FERS and the difference in program design have implications for understanding the size and path of the exposure. As shown in figure 7, as of September 30, 2012, the CSRS accrued liability is estimated at $1.2 trillion and the FERS accrued liability is $484 billion. Because of the manner in which CSRS costs are determined and funded, the system has accumulated a sizeable unfunded liability.[27] However, the unfunded liability is dealt with by the FERS Act,[28] which provides for annual credits made to the CSRDF (out of any money in the Treasury general fund not otherwise appropriated) to amortize any supplemental liability of the CSRDF with respect to current or former federal employees. Figure 7 also shows the balance of the CSRDF, which grew from $543 billion at the end of fiscal year 2001 to $820 billion at the end of fiscal year 2012.

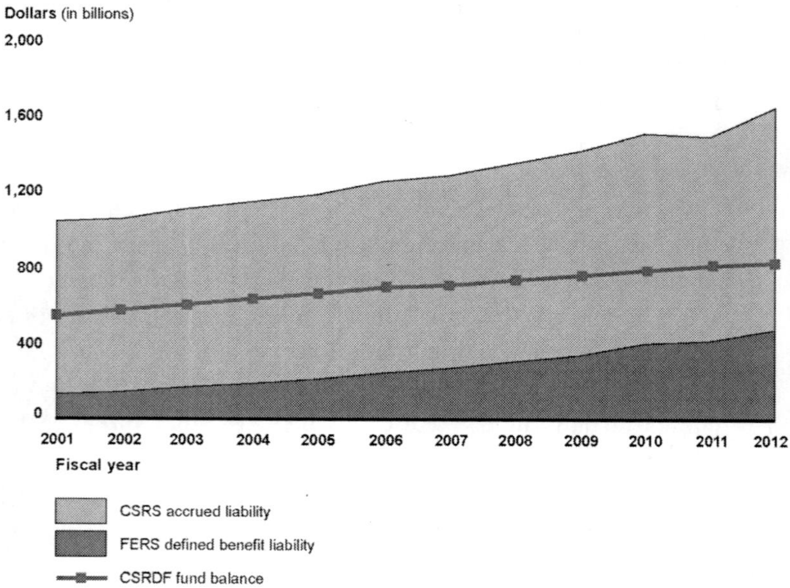

Source: GAO analysis of OPM and OMB data.

Notes: Data on liabilities from OPM's financial reports. Data on CSRDF fund balances from the President's Budget Appendix.

Figure 7. Accrued Defined Benefit Pension Liability and Trust Fund Balance, Fiscal Years 2001 through 2012.

Budget Treatment of the Exposure

Benefit payments for both CSRS and the FERS defined benefit annuity are made from the CSRDF, which has permanent, indefinite budget authority to pay benefits. Agencies pre-fund employee pensions by deferring some of their budget authority to the CSRDF, where it remains available to pay pensions to retired workers. The Treasury credits the CSRDF with budget authority in the form of special-issue securities that are backed by the full faith and credit of the U.S. government that earn interest equal to the average rate on the Treasury's outstanding long-term debt. These securities are then redeemed to make payments to retirees and survivors.

Employee contributions to the CSRDF are recorded as receipts and count as revenue to the Treasury. Payments to retirees are recorded as outlays and affect the government-wide deficit. Agency contributions are made from their appropriations and so payments toward the normal cost are visible to the individual agency, but are not reflected in the government-wide deficit because agency payments to the CSRDF are intragovernmental—that is, they are recorded as outlays by one agency and receipts by the trust fund. Treasury also makes annual payments to the CSRDF from the general fund to amortize the previously accumulated unfunded liability and to fund the difference between the CSRS employee and agency contributions and the amount that would be required to fully fund future CSRS benefits. Since no cash actually leaves the government, both agency contributions and Treasury payments to the CSRDF do not affect the government-wide deficit.

Key Factors to Consider

While the long-term exposure to the federal budget arising from civilian pension benefits is large, it is on a path to decline over time. This trend reflects both the transition from CSRS to FERS in the mid 1980s and the change to a defined contribution design and funding structure in FERS.

Civilian Post- Retirement Health Benefits

Background

Civilian annuitants are generally eligible to receive continued subsidized health benefits such as those received over the course of their working years. The Federal Employee Health Benefits program, implemented in 1960, is operated through two revolving trust funds: the Employees Health Benefits Fund and the Retired Employees Health Benefits Fund.[29] The two funds are reported jointly as the Federal Employee Health Benefits (FEHB) account in the federal budget. Under the FEHB program, the federal government pays a share of the monthly premium. The government shares the cost of the monthly premium with employees.[30]

Extent and Estimated Magnitude of the Exposure

The government's legal commitment to pay a share of the monthly premium for eligible retirees makes civilian post-retirement health benefits an explicit exposure.

The magnitude of the exposure can be estimated by the accrued liability for civilian post-retirement health benefits, which at the end of fiscal year 2012, was estimated to be $328 billion. The liability is an estimate of the government's future cost of providing post-retirement health benefits to current employees and retirees. Figure 8 shows the exposure generally grew through 2010 before declining in 2011 and 2012. As is the case with health care costs in general, estimates depend on many factors, including assumptions about utilization and health care costs far into the future and as a result, can be difficult to estimate. These variables in turn can vary with changes in covered services and participants' choice of plans.

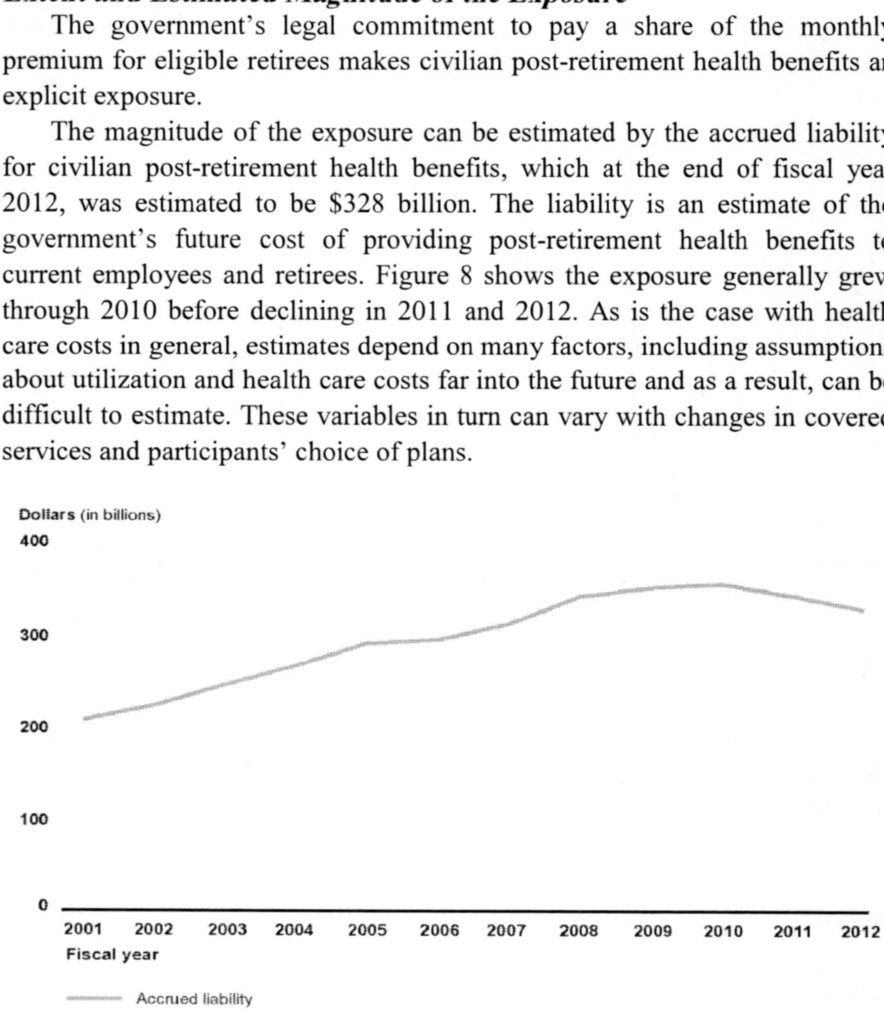

Source: GAO analysis of Treasury data.
Notes: Data from the *Financial Reports*.

Figure 8. Accrued Liability for Civilian Post-Retirement Health Benefits, Fiscal Years 2001 through 2012.

Budget Treatment of the Exposure

The FEHB Program is classified as a mandatory program and is funded through a permanent indefinite appropriation. The budget reflects payments made in the current year for both active employees and retirees. Although active and retired employees pay premiums, they do not cover the full cost. Agencies make payments to the Employees Health Benefits Fund at OPM for their share of the FEHB premiums for current employees. However, with some exceptions, the budget does not reflect the estimated costs of future payments associated with the federal government's active employees' post-retirement health benefits.[31]

Key Factors to Consider

Federal health care spending as a whole has been growing faster than the economy and is expected to continue to do so. As such it will be important to find ways to minimize costs while maintaining quality for civilian employees and retirees.

Military Pension Benefits

Background

Members of the military are eligible for a defined benefit, noncontributory pension after 20 years of active service. Active duty personnel become eligible for retirement by completing 20 years of service, regardless of age.[32] The military retirement system provides inflation-protected monthly compensation and other benefits after an active reserve or military career.[33] The system does not provide for gradual vesting; service personnel who separate prior to completing the minimum 20 years of service generally receive no retirement benefits.[34]

Since 1985, the program has operated through the Department of Defense (DOD) Military Retirement Fund and has three sources of income.[35] The first is payments from the military personnel accounts to cover most of the accruing costs of future retirement benefits being earned by today's service members (i.e., the normal cost). The second source is investment income on Treasury Securities the fund holds. The third source is made up of payments from Treasury's general fund to cover a portion of the normal cost and a portion of the previously accumulated unfunded liability, including the liability for concurrent payments to those receiving both military retired pay and disability compensation paid by the Department of Veterans Affairs (VA).[36]

Extent and Estimated Magnitude of the Exposure

The government's legal commitment to pay benefits to those retirees who reach 20 years of active service makes military pension benefits an explicit exposure.

From a government-wide perspective, the magnitude of the exposure can be estimated by the accrued liability for military pensions, which at the end of fiscal year 2012 was estimated to be $1.5 trillion, up from $708 billion in 2001 (see figure 9).

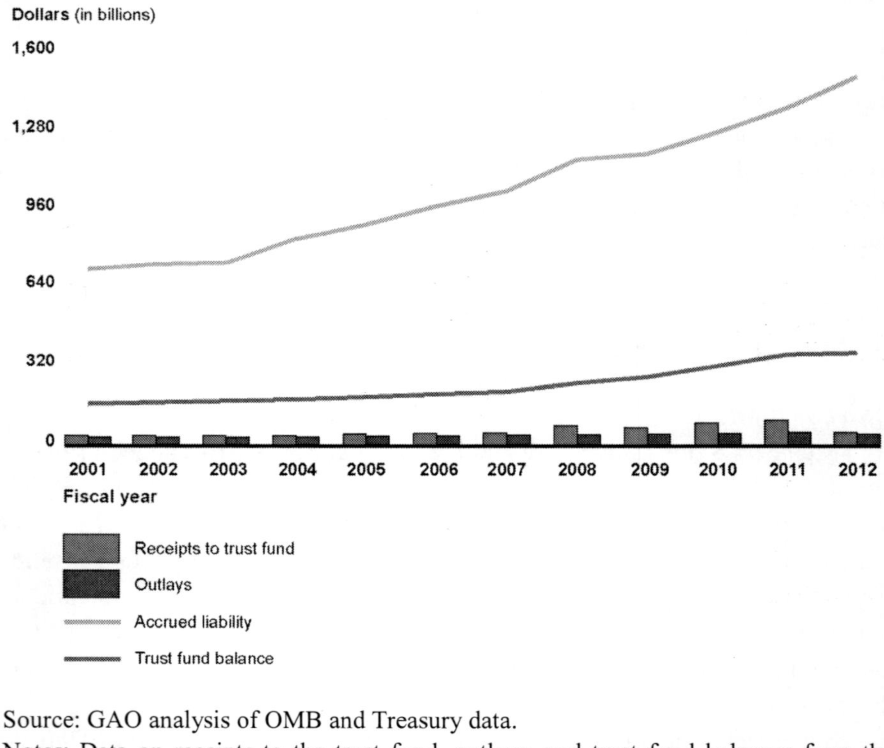

Source: GAO analysis of OMB and Treasury data.

Notes: Data on receipts to the trust fund, outlays, and trust fund balances from the President's Budget Appendix. Data on liabilities from the *Financial Reports*.

Figure 9. Military Pension Benefits Accrued Liability and Budgetary Resources in the Military Retirement Fund, Fiscal Years 2001 through 2012.

Budget Treatment of the Exposure

Figure 9 also shows the Military Retirement Fund's outlays and receipts as reported in primary budget data. Outlays reflect benefit payments to current retirees, which totaled $49 billion in 2012, up from $34 billion in 2001. Receipts to the trust fund capture the intragovernmental contributions from the services to fund future benefits earned today, Treasury general fund payments, and investment income on the Treasury Securities the fund holds. The Military Retirement Fund had assets of $376 billion as of September 30, 2012.

Beginning in 1985, military pension costs have been partially visible to DOD since it makes contributions to cover the costs as they accrue, but the normal cost is not reflected in the unified budget because the payments are intragovernmental—that is, they are recorded as outlays by one agency and receipts by the trust fund. Since no cash leaves the government, there is no effect on the government-wide deficit.

Key Factors to Consider

DOD's military compensation system, including pension benefits, is an important tool to attract and retain the number and quality of active duty servicemembers it needs to fulfill its mission. Comprehensive information about the total cost of compensation, including benefits earned today that will be paid in the future, is important for future decisions about military compensation in a constrained fiscal environment.

Military Post- Retirement Health Benefits

Background

TRICARE is DOD's managed health care system for active duty and retired uniformed service members and their families.[37] TRICARE consists of multiple plan options, a number of which cover active duty personnel, their dependents, and retirees under age 65.[38] Prior to 2001, TRICARE beneficiaries would lose their TRICARE coverage when they reached age 65, and Medicare—the federal health insurance program that provides medical benefits to elderly and disabled Americans—would become their primary health insurer. However, in 2001, the Congress expanded TRICARE by authorizing the continued provision of TRICARE benefits after age 65. The program is known as TRICARE for Life (TFL).[39] TFL provides supplementary health care coverage for TRICARE beneficiaries who are eligible for Medicare (e.g. those aged 65 or older) and pays for many services that Medicare only partially covers.[40] NonMedicare-eligible military retirees are not eligible for TFL and are covered by one of the other TRICARE programs. In addition to expanding the benefits available to Medicare-eligible retirees, the 2001 National Defense Authorization Act (NDAA) required that DOD accumulate funds in a governmental trust fund to finance the future cost of additional health benefits for Medicare-eligible retirees. This fund was started in reaction to rapidly rising health care costs. The Medicare-Eligible Retiree Health Care Fund (MERHCF) is financed through annual transfers from DOD for the future health care benefits earned by active military in that year (i.e., normal cost contributions); payments from the Treasury general fund toward the previously accumulated unfunded liability for past service; and any gains on investment income from Treasury Securities the fund holds.

Extent and Estimated Magnitude of the Exposure

The government's legal commitment to provide post-retirement medical benefits to eligible retirees makes the benefits an explicit exposure. From a government-wide perspective, the magnitude of the exposure can be estimated by the accrued liability for military post-retirement health benefits, which at the end of fiscal year 2012 was estimated to be $833 billion. The retiree health liabilities for military personnel, shown in figure 10 as the accrued liability, represents the estimated total cost of benefits earned to date for both non-Medicare eligible and Medicare-eligible retirees, as well as a portion of future benefits for those in active military service. Figure 10 also shows the balance of the MERHCF, which had assets of $176 billion at the end of fiscal year 2012.

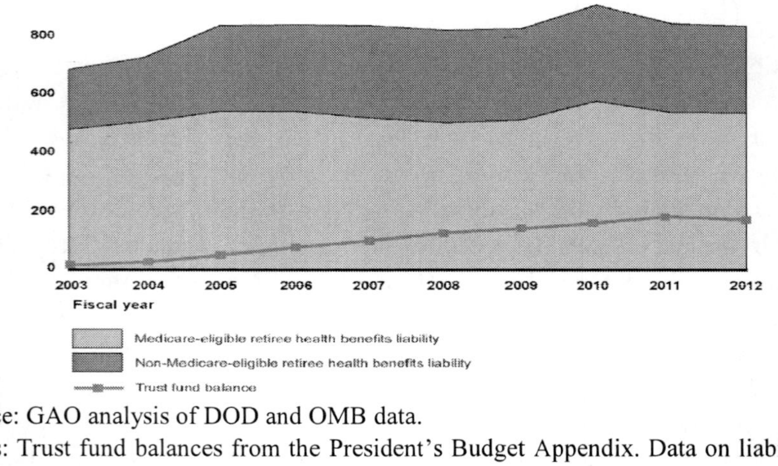

Source: GAO analysis of DOD and OMB data.

Notes: Trust fund balances from the President's Budget Appendix. Data on liabilities from the *Financial Reports*.

Figure 10. Military Post-Retirement Health Liability and Medicare-Eligible Retiree Health Care Fund Balance, Fiscal Years 2003 through 2012.

Budget Treatment of the Exposure

Beginning in 2003, current costs for Medicare-eligible military retirement benefits have been visible to DOD, since it makes contributions to cover the costs for those benefits as they are earned by current servicemembers, and the uniformed services reflect these normal cost contributions in their budgets. The Treasury also deposits funds towards the unfunded liability. Since no cash actually leaves the government from these contributions to the MERHCF, there is no effect on the government-wide cash deficit. Assets accumulating in the MERHCF are only used to pay benefits for Medicare-eligible retirees, and there is an effect on the government-wide deficit as benefits are paid from the MERHCF. In contrast, the cost of pre-Medicare-eligible post-retirement health benefits is not reflected in the uniformed services' budget data as these benefits are earned. Rather, the cost of pre-Medicare-eligible health care is paid for on a cash basis from DOD's annual Operations and Maintenance appropriation.

Key Factors to Consider

We have highlighted a range of long-standing issues surrounding DOD's Medical Healthcare System. As health care consumes an increasingly larger portion of the defense budget, DOD leadership has recognized the need to reduce duplication and overhead to operate the most efficient health system possible. In 2012, we reported that DOD had identified initiatives aimed at slowing its rising health care costs, but its ability to implement and monitor these initiatives and achieve related costs savings is limited.[41]

Veterans Compensation

Background

The federal government provides benefits to eligible veterans and their survivors to compensate for the loss of potential earnings due to service-connected disability or death. Entitlement to compensation depends on the veteran's disabilities having been incurred in, or aggravated during, active military service; death while on duty; or death resulting from service-connected disabilities.[42] These benefits can be in place of (or in combination with) the DOD military retired pay.[43]

Extent and Estimated Magnitude of the Exposure

The government's legal commitment to provide compensation to eligible veterans makes veterans compensation payments an explicit exposure.

The magnitude of the exposure can be estimated by the accrued liability, which at the end of fiscal year 2012 was estimated to be $1.8 trillion. This measure reflects the present value of expected future payments to current veterans already receiving compensation payments, to veterans who are not currently receiving compensation but will in the future, and to a portion of those in active military service assumed by the VA to become eligible for compensation in the future. Figure 11 illustrates the growth in this exposure, which more than doubled between 2001 and 2012—from $692 billion to $1.8 trillion—and represents the fastest rate of growth among the compensation programs we examined in this report. The annual growth of the accrued liability, which averaged about $97 billion from fiscal years 2001 to 2012, reflects increases in the number of veterans as a result of wars and other conflicts, the aging of the veteran population, and changes in the benefits and services provided to veterans.

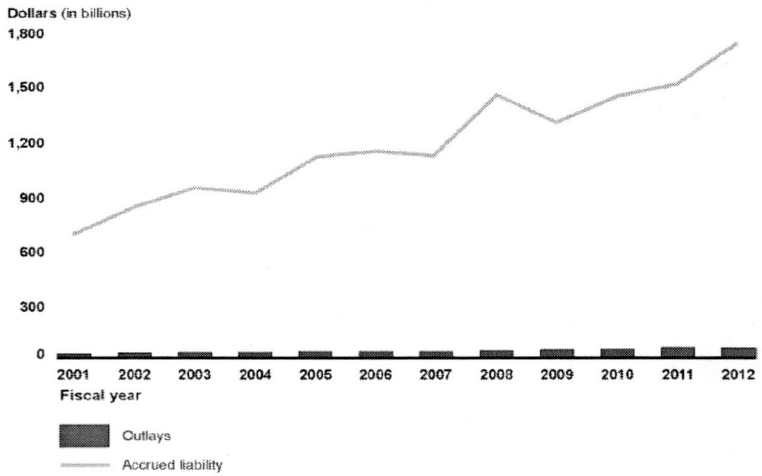

Source: GAO analysis of OMB and Treasury data.

Note: Outlays in this figure from the President's Budget Appendix and reflect not only payments for veterans compensation but also veterans pension benefits and burial benefits. Pension and burial benefits represent a relatively small portion of outlays. Data on liabilities from the *Financial Reports*.

Figure 11. Veterans Compensation and Pensions Liability and Annual Outlays, Fiscal Years 2001 through 2012.

Budget Treatment of the Exposure

Veterans Compensation and Pensions annually receives no-year funds through regular appropriations. Figure 11 also shows the program's annual outlays as reported in primary budget data. Outlays, which increased from $21 billion in fiscal year 2001 to $55 billion in fiscal year 2012, reflect payments made to current veterans. However, the budget does not reflect the estimated costs of future payments earned by current service.

Key Factors to Consider

The VA's Veterans Compensation and Pensions account funds one of the largest federal disability programs. In the years ahead, enrollment in the VA's disability compensation program could increase given the conflicts in Iraq and Afghanistan and as more Vietnam veterans—a significant portion of the total veteran population—further age into disability-prone years.[44] These trends directly affect the extent and magnitude of the government's fiscal exposure arising from veterans compensation. Further, since 2003, veterans compensation and other federal disability programs have been on our High Risk List, due in part to challenges agencies face in keeping their criteria for evaluating disability and determining compensation consistent with advances in medicine, technology, and changes in the labor market and society.[45]

End Notes

[1] For purposes of this report, the term legal commitment refers to the government's responsibility for future financial obligations.

[2] GAO, *Fiscal Exposures: Improving the Budgetary Focus on Long-Term Costs and Uncertainties,* GAO-03-213 (Washington, D.C.: Jan. 24, 2003).

[3] The term "budget" can refer to a variety of plans, including the President's budget, the congressional budget resolution or an agency's budget documents. In this report, we focused on reporting in the President's budget. *See*, 31 U.S.C. § 1105.

[4] The *Financial Report* is prepared by the Department of the Treasury, in coordination with the Office of Management and Budget (OMB). Generally, a cost is recorded in the *Financial Report* on an accrual basis—when the obligation is incurred rather than when it is paid; as such costs for some programs are recognized earlier than in the budget, which generally measures outlays on a cash or cash-equivalent basis.

[5] The budget reflected contributions to a trust fund from the Department of Defense for TRICARE for Life as of 2003.

[6] Federal trust funds are used to link earmarked receipts with the expenditures of those receipts for a dedicated purpose. For example, monies in the Civil Service Retirement and Disability Fund and Military Retirement Fund are dedicated to fund long-term pension commitments. Fund balances stem from a combination of receipts and appropriated contributions from the general fund, which include interest payments and the employer share of federal employee

pension costs. See GAO, *Federal Trust and Other Earmarked Funds: Answers to Frequently Asked Questions,* GAO-01-199SP (Washington, D.C.: Jan. 2001). Data for civilian pension liabilities were obtained from the Office of Personnel Management's (OPM) financial reports.

[7] GAO, *Long-Term Commitments: Improving the Budgetary Focus on Environmental Liabilities,* GAO-03-219 (Washington, D.C.: Jan. 24, 2003) and *Budget Issues: Budgeting for Federal Insurance Programs,* GAO/AIMD-97-16 (Washington, D.C.: Sept. 30, 1997).

[8] GAO, *Budget Issues: Accrual Budgeting Useful in Certain Areas but Does Not Provide Sufficient Information for Reporting on Our Nation's Longer-Term Fiscal Challenge*, GAO-08-206 (Washington, D.C.: Dec. 2007); and GAO, *Accrual Budgeting: Experiences of Other Nations and Implications for the United States,* GAO/AIMD-00-57 (Washington, D.C.: Feb. 18, 2000).

[9] GAO, *Mandatory Spending: Using Budget Triggers to Constrain Growth*, GAO-06-276 (Washington, D.C.: Jan. 31, 2006); and GAO, *Budget Policy: Issues in Capping Mandatory Spending*, GAO/AIMD-94-155 (Washington, D.C.: Jul. 18, 1994).

[10] GAO-03-213.

[11] Social insurance programs are generally defined as government programs intended to protect households or individuals against certain social risks including loss of income. In contrast to other federal insurance programs, these programs are generally viewed as transfer payments, which are benefits provided without requiring the recipient to provide current or future goods or services of equivalent value in return. In this respect, they are different from pension and other employee compensation that is provided in exchange for services.

[12] GAO, *The Federal Government's Long-Term Fiscal Outlook: Spring 2013 Update,* GAO-13-481SP, (Washington, D.C.: Apr. 11, 2013). These figures also include spending for other federal health programs delivered through the states – the Children's Health Insurance Program and the subsidies available to assist individuals to purchase insurance coverage through the American Health Benefit Exchanges.

[13] See Congressional Budget Office, *The 2012 Long-Term Budget Outlook* (Washington, D.C.: Jun. 5, 2012) and Office of Management and Budget, *Analytical Perspectives, Budget of the U.S. Government, Fiscal Year 2014* (Washington, D.C., Apr. 10, 2013).

[14] See appendix I for information on the extent and estimated magnitude of these fiscal exposures.

[15] PBGC is a wholly-owned corporation of the U.S. government. Its financial activities are included in the federal budget and consolidated financial statement of the U.S. government. PBGC is required to be self-financing and does not receive funds from the general fund of the Treasury. See appendix I for more details.

[16] The Federal Housing Finance Regulatory Reform Act of 2008 established the Federal Housing Finance Agency (FHFA), which was created to enhance authority over these GSEs and provide the Secretary of the Treasury with certain authorities intended to ensure the financial stability of these GSEs. Treasury entered into a Senior Preferred Stock Purchase Agreement (hereafter referred to as the agreements) with each GSE. The agreements, which have no expiration date, provide that Treasury will disburse funds to these GSEs if at the end of any quarter the FHFA determines that the liabilities of either GSE exceed its assets.

[17] Budget authority is the authority to incur obligations and pay expenses.

[18] For more information on this concept, see GAO/AIMD-97-16 or GAO, *Budget Issues: Budgeting for Federal Insurance Programs*, GAO/T-AIMD-98-147 (Washington, D.C.: Apr. 23, 1998).

[19] PBGC operates two insurance programs—one for single employer plans and another for multiemployer plans, which are created by collective bargaining agreements and include

more than one employer. Operations are financed by premiums, assets from terminated plans, and investment income. While the single employer program is supported by both premiums and an asset base, the multiemployer program is supported mainly by premiums and a relatively small asset base. Because of long-term challenges related to PBGC's governance and funding structure, PBGC's financial future is uncertain. See GAO, *High-Risk Series: An Update*, GAO-13-283 (Washington, D.C.: Feb. 2013).

[20] GAO, *Federal Trust and Other Earmarked Funds: Answers to Frequently Asked Questions*, GAO-01-199SP (Washington, D.C.: Jan. 2001).

[21] The Biggert-Waters Flood Insurance Reform Act of 2012, Pub. L. No. 112-141, requires the subsidized premiums be eliminated and actuarially sound premiums phased in.

[22] GAO, *GAO's High Risk Program*, GAO-06-497T, (Washington, D.C.: March 15, 2006).

[23] GAO-13-283.

[24] GAO-01-199SP.

[25] Borrowing authority permits an agency to borrow money, usually from the Treasury, then obligate against amounts borrowed.

[26] Biggert-Waters Flood Insurance Reform Act of 2012, Pub. L. No. 112-141, § §100205, 100207.

[27] GAO-08-206. Other countries we reviewed—Australia, New Zealand, the Netherlands, and United Kingdom—use accrual budgeting more extensively to support broader efforts to improve the efficiency and performance of the public sector. However, none of these other countries used accrual budgeting for social insurance programs.

[28] The risk assumed can be difficult to measure for many federal activities, but is most clearly identifiable in federal insurance programs.

End Notes for Appendix I

[1] We use the term general fund to refer to the account in the U.S. Treasury holding all federal money not allocated by law to any other fund account and from which appropriations are generally drawn.

[2] GAO-13-283.

[3] The President's Budget Appendix reports supplemental information for federal insurance programs, including a balance sheet for NFIP. NFIP's net position is recorded in the balance sheet.

[4] GAO-13-283.

[5] AECOM, *The Impact of Climate Change and Population Growth on the National Flood Insurance Program Through 2100,* (June 2013).

[6] The Biggert-Waters Flood Insurance Reform Act of 2012, Pub. L. No. 112-141.

[7] Pub. L. No. 93-406, § 4002(a)

[8] Generally speaking, a claim occurs when a plan sponsor with an underfunded plan goes bankrupt and the plan is terminated.

[9] Congress recently repealed section 4005(c) of the Employee Retirement Investment Security Act, which provided authority for the PBGC's federal line of credit up to $100 million. *See* the Moving Ahead for Progress in the 21st Century Act (MAP-21), Pub. L. No. 112-141, § 40234 (a).

[10] For further discussion, see GAO, *Private Pensions: Timely Action Needed to Address Impending Multiemployer Plan Insolvencies*, GAO-13-240, (Washington, D.C.: Mar. 28, 2013).

[11] GAO, *Pension Benefit Guaranty Corporation: Redesigned Premium Structure Could Better Align Rates With Risk From Plan Sponsors*, GAO-13-58, (Washington, D.C.: Nov. 7, 2012) and Pension Benefit Guaranty Corporation, *Excellence in Customer Service: Annual Report 2012*, (Washington, D.C.: Nov.14, 2012).

[12] GAO-13-58.

[13] Dividends received by Treasury under this agreement are reflected in the general fund.

[14] GAO, *Fannie Mae and Freddie Mac: Analysis of Options for Revising the Housing Enterprises' Long-term Structures,* GAO-09-782, (Washington, D.C.: Sept. 10, 2009).

[15] Pub. L. No. 101-508. Under the Federal Credit Reform Act of 1990, the credit subsidy cost of direct loans and loan guarantees is the net present value of the estimated longterm cost to the government at the time the credit is provided of such programs, less administrative expenses. The act was intended to improve disclosures about the risks associated with government direct loans and guarantee programs and assist Congress in making budget decisions about such programs.

[16] CSRS was authorized by the Civil Service Retirement Act of 1920 (Pub. L. No. 66-215) and FERS was established by the Federal Employees' Retirement System Act of 1986 (Pub. L. No. 99-335).

[17] In a defined benefit plan, the retirement benefit typically is based on a formula specified in the plan, which will often be based on factors such as an employee's years of service, age at retirement, and wages or salary. For a civilian employee retiring after 30 years of federal service, a CSRS annuity will be equal to 56.25 percent of the average of the highest three consecutive years of basic pay. A FERS employee retiring at the age of 62 with 30 years of service will receive a FERS annuity equal to 33 percent of the average of the highest three consecutive years of pay.

[18] Some CSRS employees will have paid or will pay Social Security for employment outside the federal government.

[19] The TSP is a defined contribution retirement plan similar to the 401(k) plans provided by many employers in the private sector. The income that a retired worker receives from the TSP will depend on the balance in his or her account. Contributions of up to 5 percent of pay made by FERS employees are matched by the federal government. CSRS employees can contribute to the TSP, but they receive no matching contributions. The TSP is non-budgetary and agency matching contributions are recorded as outlays.

[20] All CSRDF investments are in U.S. Treasury and Federal Financing Bank securities and are therefore classified as intragovernmental. The government does not set aside assets to pay future benefits or other expenditures associated with designated funds. Throughout this report, we refer to all funds generated through the investment of assets as investment income.

[21] According to the 2012 *Financial Report*, other significant civilian pension plans include those of the Coast Guard, Foreign Service, Tennessee Valley Authority, U.S. Postal Service, and the Department of Health and Human Services.

[22] FERS currently covers the majority of active civilian employees. As of fiscal year 2012, there were 323,000 active employees covered by CSRS compared to 2,493,000 active FERS employees.

[23] According to the Congressional Budget Office, in fiscal year 2012 the average monthly benefit for FERS annuitants was $1,147 compared to an average monthly benefit of $3,123 for

CSRS annuitants. Congressional Budget Office, March 2012 Baseline for the Civil Service Retirement and Disability Fund.

[24] The U.S. Postal Service is an exception. Separate CSRS funding provisions were enacted under Pub. L. No. 108-18, requiring the Postal Service to contribute the normal-cost percentage to CSRS, which means the entry-age normal cost computed by the Office of Personnel Management in accordance with generally accepted actuarial practice and standards (using dynamic assumptions) and expressed as a level of percentage of aggregate basic pay. The Postal Service was also required to finance any unfunded liabilities. Under the Postal Accountability and Enhancement Act, Pub. L. No. 109-435, the Postal Service, beginning in 2017, must amortize any additional unfunded actuarial liabilities which may arise. Currently, Postal CSRS employees contribute 7 percent of pay.

[25] Normal cost, an actuarial concept used in pension and other post-retirement benefit cost calculations, is the discounted present value of the cost to pay benefits in the future attributable to employees' current year of service. If the normal costs for specific beneficiaries are accumulated during all years of service in which benefits are earned, and all actuarial assumptions are met, the sum accumulated will pay for the benefits as they come due.

[26] The Middle Class Tax Relief and Job Creation Act of 2012 (Pub. L. No. 112-96) provided for increased employee contributions of 3.1 percent of pay to the CSRDF for employees hired after December 31, 2012.

[27] The term "unfunded liability" has been used to refer to gaps between the projected financial commitment to a program or expenditure and the earmarked revenues that are expected to be available to fund that commitment. However, no federal obligation can be truly considered "unfunded" because of the government's sovereign power to tax to meet its obligations.

[28] Pub. L. No. 99-335

[29] After age 65, the retirees' FEHB benefits are coordinated with Medicare benefits.

[30] The government's share for annuitants and current employees is 72 percent of the weighted average of the premiums for all participating plans, with a cap of 75 percent of the total premium.

[31] The U.S. Patent and Trademark Office is an exception; since 2005 it has made accrual payments to the FEHB fund associated with its active employees' post-retirement health benefits. In addition, since 2006, the U.S. Postal Service is required to make scheduled prefunding contributions to the Postal Service Retiree Health Benefit Fund in the budget. However, the Postal Service has not made required payments of $11.1 billion due in fiscal year 2012. See GAO, *U.S. Postal Service: Proposed Health Plan Could Improve Financial Condition, but Impact on Medicare and Other Issues Should Be Weighed Before Approval*, GAO-13-658 (Washington, D.C., July 18, 2013) and *U.S. Postal Service: Status, Financial Outlook, and Alternative Approaches to Fund Retiree Health Benefits*, GAO-13-112 (Washington, D.C., Dec. 4, 2012).

[32] Members of the reserves may retire after 20 qualifying years of creditable service, but reserve retired pay is not payable until age 60, with some exceptions.

[33] Since 2001, service members also have been eligible to participate in the federal Thrift Savings Plan, the defined-contribution plan available to civilian employees, although generally without any matching contributions from the government.

[34] The military retirement system applies to members of the Army, Navy, Marine Corps and Air Force. Most of the provisions also apply to retirement systems for members of the Coast Guard (administered by the Department of Homeland Security), officers of the Public

Health Service (administered by the Department of Health and Human Services), and officers of the National Oceanic and Atmospheric Administration (administered by the Department of Commerce).

[35] Pub. L. No. 98-94 provided for accrual funding of the military retirement system and for the establishment of a Department of Defense Military Retirement Fund in 1985.

[36] Concurrent receipt refers to the simultaneous receipt of military retired pay and VA disability compensation. Prior to 2004, the law required that military retired pay be reduced dollar-for-dollar by the amount of any VA disability compensation received (e.g. an offset). The 2004 National Defense Authorization Act (Pub. L. No. 108-136) authorized concurrent receipt of both amounts without a required offset for certain military retirees.

[37] The uniformed services include the U.S. Army, U.S. Air Force, U.S. Navy, U.S. Marine Corps, U.S. Coast Guard, the Commissioned Corps of the Public Health Service, and the Commissioned Corps of the National Oceanic and Atmospheric Association.

[38] DOD provides health care benefits to its non-Medicare-eligible beneficiary population through several TRICARE options.

[39] The National Defense Authorization Act for Fiscal Year 2001, Pub. L. No. 106-398 established the Department of Defense Medicare-Eligible Retiree Health Care Fund, administered by the Secretary of the Treasury.

[40] While TRICARE beneficiaries over age 65 do not have to pay for their TFL coverage, they must be eligible for Medicare Part A and elect to carry Medicare Part B. Retired TRICARE beneficiaries are required to pay premiums for Medicare Part B, which covers certain physician, outpatient hospital, laboratory, and other services. TFL covers out-of-pocket costs incurred by beneficiaries for care over the sum of the amount paid for under Medicare.

[41] GAO, *Defense Health Care: Applying Key Management Practices Should Help Achieve Efficiencies within the Military Health System*, GAO-12-224 (Washington, D.C.: Apr. 12, 2012).

[42] Burial benefits are also provided and include a burial and plot or internment allowance payable for a veteran who, at the time of death, is qualified to receive compensation or pension, or whose death occurred in a VA facility.

[43] Prior to 2004, the law required that military retired pay be reduced dollar-for-dollar by the amount of any VA disability compensation received (e.g. an offset). The 2004 National Defense Authorization Act (Pub. L. No.108-136) authorized actual concurrent receipt, or the simultaneous receipt of military retired pay and VA disability compensation for certain military retirees.

[44] GAO, *VA Disability Compensation: Action Needed to Address Hurdles Facing Program Modernization*, GAO-12-846 (Washington, D.C.: Sept. 10, 2012).

[45] GAO-13-283.

In: Fiscal Exposures
Editor: Landon P. Merrill

ISBN: 978-1-63463-589-9

Chapter 2

BUDGET ISSUES: OPPORTUNITIES TO REDUCE FEDERAL FISCAL EXPOSURES THROUGH GREATER RESILIENCE TO CLIMATE CHANGE AND EXTREME WEATHER*

Alfredo Gomez

WHY GAO DID THIS STUDY

Certain types of extreme weather events have become more frequent or intense according to the United States Global Change Research Program, including prolonged periods of heat, heavy downpours, and, in some regions, floods and droughts. While it is not possible to link any individual weather event to climate change, the impacts of these events affect many sectors of our economy, including the budgets of federal, state, and local governments.

GAO focuses particular attention on government operations it identifies as posing a "high risk" to the American taxpayer and, in February 2013, added to its High Risk List the area *Limiting the Federal Government's Fiscal*

* This is an edited, reformatted and augmented version of a report, GAO-14-504T, issued by the U.S. Government Accountability Office, July 29, 2014. This report was originally presented as testimony before the Senate Committee on the Budget. Alfredo Gomez is Director of Natural Resources and Environment at the GAO.

Exposure by Better Managing Climate Change Risks. GAO's past work has identified a variety of fiscal exposures—responsibilities, programs, and activities that may explicitly or implicitly expose the federal government to future spending.

This testimony is based on reports GAO issued from August 2007 to May 2014, and discusses (1) federal fiscal exposures resulting from climate-related and extreme weather impacts on critical infrastructure and federal lands, and (2) how improved federal technical assistance to all levels of government can help reduce climate-related fiscal exposures.

GAO is not making new recommendations but has made numerous recommendations in prior reports on this topic, which are in varying states of implementation by the Executive Office of the President and federal agencies.

WHAT GAO FOUND

Climate change and related extreme weather impacts on infrastructure and federal lands increase fiscal exposures that the federal budget does not fully reflect. Investing in resilience—actions to reduce potential future losses rather than waiting for an event to occur and paying for recovery afterward—can reduce the potential impacts of climate-related events. Implementing resilience measures creates additional up-front costs but could also confer benefits, such as a reduction in future damages from climate-related events. Key examples of vulnerable infrastructure and federal lands GAO has identified include:

- *Department of Defense (DOD) facilities.* DOD manages a global real-estate portfolio that includes over 555,000 facilities and 28 million acres of land with a replacement value DOD estimates at close to $850 billion. This infrastructure is vulnerable to the potential impacts of climate change and related extreme weather events. For example, in May 2014, GAO reported that a military base in the desert Southwest experienced a rain event in August 2013 in which about 1 year's worth of rain fell in 80 minutes. The flooding caused by the storm damaged more than 160 facilities, 8 roads, 1 bridge, and 11,000 linear feet of fencing, resulting in an estimated $64 million in damages.
- *Other large federal facilities.* The federal government owns and operates hundreds of thousands of other facilities that a changing climate could affect. For example, the National Aeronautics and

Space Administration (NASA) manages more than 5,000 buildings and other structures. GAO reported in April 2013 that, in total, these NASA assets—many of which are in coastal areas vulnerable to storm surge and sea level rise—represent more than $32 billion in current replacement value.

- *Federal lands*. The federal government manages nearly 30 percent of the land in the United States—about 650 million acres of land—including 401 national park units and 155 national forests. GAO reported in May 2013 that these resources are vulnerable to changes in the climate, including the possibility of more frequent and severe droughts and wildfires. Appropriations for federal wildland fire management activities have tripled since 1999, averaging over $3 billion annually in recent years.

GAO has reported that improved climate-related technical assistance to all levels of government can help limit federal fiscal exposures. The federal government invests tens of billions of dollars annually in infrastructure projects that state and local governments prioritize, such as roads and bridges. Total public spending on transportation and water infrastructure exceeds $300 billion annually, with about 25 percent coming from the federal government and the rest from state and local governments. GAO's April 2013 report on infrastructure adaptation concluded that the federal government could help state and local efforts to increase their resilience by (1) improving access to and use of available climate-related information, (2) providing officials with improved access to technical assistance, and (3) helping officials consider climate change in their planning processes.

* * *

Chairman Murray, Ranking Member Sessions, and Members of the Committee:

I am pleased to be here today to discuss our work on reducing federal fiscal exposures posed by climate change and extreme weather events.[1] Climate change affects the American people in far-reaching ways, according to the National Research Council (NRC) and the United States Global Change Research Program's (USGCRP) May 2014 National Climate Assessment.[2] Certain types of extreme weather events with links to climate change have become more frequent or intense according to NRC and USGCRP, including prolonged periods of heat; heavy downpours; and, in some regions, floods and droughts. In addition, according to NRC and USGCRP, warming causes sea level to rise, sea ice to melt, and oceans to become more acidic as they absorb carbon dioxide. While it is not possible to link any individual weather event to climate change, these and other observed impacts of such events disrupt people's lives and affect many sectors of our economy, including the budgets of federal, state, and local governments.

Extreme weather events have cost the nation tens of billions of dollars in damages over the past decade. In 2012, for example, Superstorm Sandy alone caused tens of billions of dollars in damages to buildings, utilities, transportation systems, and other infrastructure. Heavy rainfall and snowfall events (which increase the risk of flooding) and heatwaves are generally becoming more frequent, consistent with theoretical expectations for a warmer and moister atmosphere due to changes in the climate, according to a February 2014 joint report by the U.S. National Academy of Sciences and the Royal Society in the United Kingdom.[3] The federal budget, however, generally does not account for disaster assistance provided in cases such as Superstorm Sandy—for which Congress provided about $60 billion in budget authority for such assistance—or the long-term impacts of climate change on existing federal infrastructure and programs.[4] Because of these significant financial risks and the nation's fiscal condition, in February 2013, we added *Limiting the Federal Government's Fiscal Exposure by Better Managing Climate Change Risks* to our list of high-risk areas.[5]

One way to reduce the potential impacts of climate change is to invest in enhancing resilience. The National Academies define resilience as the ability to prepare and plan for, absorb, recover from, and more successfully adapt to adverse events.[6] As we reported in April 2013, enhanced resilience results from actions to reduce potential future losses, rather than waiting for an event to occur and paying for recovery afterward.[7] Enhancing resilience has begun to receive more attention because greenhouse gases that are in the atmosphere could continue altering the climate system into the future, regardless of efforts to control emissions.

Implementing resilience measures creates additional up-front costs but could also confer benefits, such as a reduction in future damages from climate-related events. Federal efforts have begun to focus on enhancing resilience and providing information to state and local decision makers so they can make more informed decisions about fiscal exposure to potential climate-related events.[8] Decisions to adapt infrastructure to climate change can also depend on many other factors, such as the availability of substitutes or the remaining useful life of existing infrastructure.

My testimony today discusses (1) federal fiscal exposures resulting from climate-related and extreme weather impacts on critical infrastructure and federal lands, and (2) how improved federal technical assistance to all levels of government can help reduce climate-related fiscal exposures. My testimony is based on reports we issued from August 2007 to May 2014. Detailed information on our scope and methodology for our prior work can be found in those reports. The work this testimony is based on was conducted in accordance with generally accepted government auditing standards. Those standards require that we plan and perform the audit to obtain sufficient, appropriate evidence to provide a reasonable basis for our findings and conclusions based on our audit objectives. We believe that the evidence obtained provides a reasonable basis for our findings and conclusions based on our audit objectives.

Climate-Related and Extreme Weather Impacts on Infrastructure and Federal Lands Increase Federal Fiscal Exposures

As our past work has found, climate-related and extreme weather impacts on physical infrastructure such as buildings, roads, and bridges, as well as on federal lands, increase federal fiscal exposures. Infrastructure is typically designed to withstand and operate within historical climate patterns. However, according to NRC, as the climate changes, historical patterns do not provide reliable predictions of the future, in particular, those related to extreme weather events.[9] Thus, infrastructure designs may underestimate potential climate-related impacts over their design life, which can range up to 50 to 100 years. Federal agencies responsible for the long-term management of federal lands face similar impacts. Climate-related impacts can increase the operating and maintenance costs of infrastructure and federal lands or decrease the infrastructure's life span, leading to increased fiscal exposures for the federal government that are not fully reflected in the budget. Key examples from our recent work include (1) Department of Defense (DOD) facilities, (2) other large federal facilities such as National Aeronautics and Space Administration (NASA) centers, and (3) federal lands such as National Parks.

DOD Facilities

DOD manages a global real-estate portfolio that includes over 555,000 facilities and 28 million acres of land with a replacement value that DOD estimates at close to $850 billion. Within the United States, the department's extensive infrastructure of bases and training ranges— critical to maintaining military readiness—extends across the country, including Alaska and Hawaii. DOD incurs substantial costs for infrastructure, with a base budget for military construction and family housing totaling more than $9.8 billion in fiscal year 2014. As we reported in May 2014, this infrastructure is vulnerable to the potential impacts of climate change, including increased drought and more frequent and severe extreme weather events in certain locations.[10]

In its 2014 Quadrennial Defense Review, DOD stated that the impacts of climate change may increase the frequency, scale, and complexity of future missions, while undermining the capacity of domestic installations to support training activities. For example, in our May 2014 report on DOD infrastructure adaptation, we found that drought contributed to wildfires at an Army installation in Alaska that delayed certain units' training (see fig. 1).[11] Further, the fire limited the use of certain weapons systems in training and decreased the realism of the training.

Our May 2014 report also found that more frequent and more severe extreme weather events may result in increased fiscal exposure for DOD. Extreme precipitation events may lead to potential vulnerabilities such as increased maintenance costs for roads, utilities, and runways and increased flood-control measures. For example, we reported that in August 2013, a military base in the desert Southwest experienced an extreme rain event in which approximately 1 year's worth of rain fell in 80 minutes. According to Army officials and documents, the flooding caused by the storm damaged more than 160 facilities, 8 roads, 1 bridge, and 11,000 linear feet of fencing and resulted in an estimated $64 million in damage. Figure 2 shows flood damage to guard towers from this event.

Other Large Federal Facilities

The federal government owns and operates hundreds of thousands of non-defense buildings and facilities that a changing climate could affect. For example, NASA's real property holdings include more than 5,000 buildings and other structures such as wind tunnels, laboratories, launch pads, and test stands. In total, these NASA assets—many of which are located in vulnerable coastal areas—represent more than $32 billion in current replacement value.

Source: Alaska Fire Service. GAO-14-504T.

Note: Drought conditions contributed to a 2013 fire that limited the use of certain weapons systems and training activities.

Figure 1. Wildfire on a DOD Training Range in Alaska.

Source: U.S. Army. GAO-14-504T.

Note: Guard towers at an Army training area in the Southwestern United States (left); The same type of guard tower, toppled and severely damaged by flash flooding from an extreme precipitation event at this training area (right).

Figure 2. Army Training Area in Southwestern United States.

Our April 2013 report on infrastructure adaptation showed the vulnerability of Johnson Space Center and its mission control center, often referred to as the nerve center for America's human space program.[12] As shown in figure 3, the center is located in Houston, Texas, near Galveston Bay and the Gulf of Mexico. Johnson Space Center's facilities—conservatively valued at $2.3 billion—are vulnerable to storm surge and sea level rise because of their location on the Gulf Coast.

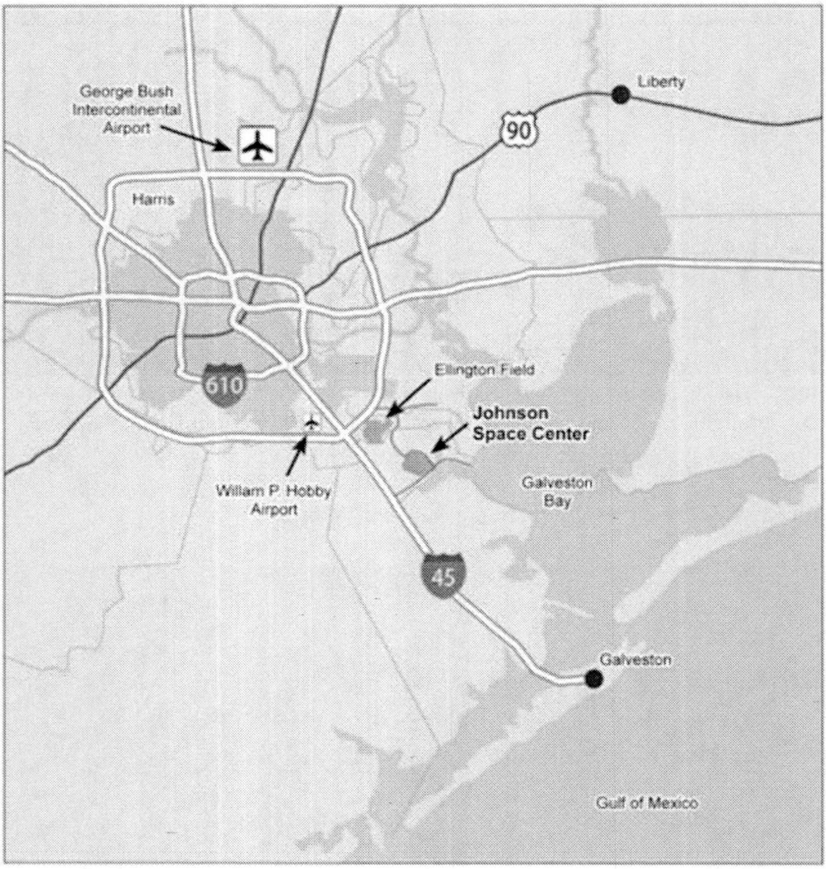

Source: NASA. GAO-14-504T.

Figure 3. Location of Johnson Space Center.

Federal Lands

The federal government manages nearly 30 percent of the land in the United States for a variety of purposes, such as recreation, grazing, timber, and habitat for fish and wildlife. Specifically, federal agencies manage natural resources on about 650 million acres of land, including 401 national park units and 155 national forests. As we reported in May 2013, these resources are vulnerable to changes in the climate, including increases in air and water temperatures, wildfires, and drought; forests stressed by drought becoming more vulnerable to insect infestations; rising sea levels; and reduced snow cover and retreating glaciers.[13] In addition, various species are expected to be at risk of becoming extinct due to the loss of habitat critical to their survival. Many of these changes have already been observed on federally managed lands and waters and are expected to continue, and one of the areas where the federal government's fiscal exposure is expected to increase is in its role as the manager of large amounts of land and other natural resources. According to USGCRP's May 2014 National Climate Assessment, hotter and drier weather and earlier snowmelt mean that wildfires in the West start earlier in the spring, last later into the fall, and burn more acres.[14] Appropriations for the federal government's wildland fire management activities have tripled, averaging over $3 billion annually in recent years, up from about $1 billion in fiscal year 1999.[15]

Improved Climate-Related Technical Assistance to All Levels of Government Can Help Limit Federal Fiscal Exposures

As we have previously reported, improved climate-related technical assistance to all levels of government can help limit federal fiscal exposures. Existing federal efforts encourage a decentralized approach to such assistance, with federal agencies incorporating climate-related information into their planning, operations, policies, and programs and establishing their own methods for collecting, storing, and disseminating climate-related data. Reflecting this approach, technical assistance from the federal government to state and local governments also exists in an uncoordinated confederation of networks and institutions. As we reported in our February 2015 high-risk update, the challenge is to develop a cohesive approach at the federal level that also informs action at the state and local levels.[16]

Federal Decision Makers

The Executive Office of the President and federal agencies have many efforts underway to increase the resilience of federal infrastructure and programs. For example, executive orders issued in 2009 and 2013 directed agencies to create climate change adaptation plans which integrate consideration of climate change into their operations and overall mission objectives, including the costs and benefits of improving climate adaptation and resilience with real-property investments and construction of new facilities.[17]

Recognizing these and many other emerging efforts, our prior work shows that federal decision makers still need help understanding how to build resilience into their infrastructure and planning processes. For example, in our May 2014 report, we found that DOD requires selected infrastructure planning efforts for existing and future infrastructure to account for climate change impacts, but its planners did not have key information necessary to make decisions that account for climate and related risks.[18] We recommended that DOD provide further information to installation planners and clarify actions that account for climate change in planning documents. DOD concurred with our recommendations.

Previously, in 2007, we concluded that federal resource management agencies had not made climate change a high priority and did not have specific guidance in place advising their managers on addressing the effects of climate change in their resource management. [19] As a result, we recommended that that the Secretaries of Agriculture, Commerce, and the Interior develop guidance for their resource managers that explains how they expect to address the effects of climate change, and the three departments generally agreed with this recommendation. However, as we found in our May 2013 report, resource managers still struggled to incorporate climate-related information into their day-to-day activities, even with the creation of strategic policy documents and high-level agency guidance.[20]

State and Local Decision Makers

The federal government invests tens of billions of dollars annually in infrastructure projects prioritized and supervised by state and local governments. In total, the United States has about 4 million miles of roads and 30,000 wastewater treatment and collection facilities. According to a 2010

Congressional Budget Office report, total public spending on transportation and water infrastructure exceeds $300 billion annually, with roughly 25 percent of this amount coming from the federal government and the rest coming from state and local governments.[21] However, the federal government plays a limited role in project-level planning for transportation and wastewater infrastructure, and state and local efforts to consider climate change in infrastructure planning have occurred primarily on a limited, ad hoc basis. The federal government has a key interest in helping state and local decision makers increase their resilience to climate change and extreme weather events because uninsured losses may increase the federal government's fiscal exposure through federal disaster assistance programs.

Louisiana State Highway 1 is an example of infrastructure of national importance that is managed by state and local governments. Our April 2013 report on infrastructure adaptation found that according to National Oceanic and Atmospheric Administration estimates, within 15 years, segments of Louisiana State Highway 1 will be inundated by tides an average of 30 times annually due to relative sea level rise. 22 Louisiana Highway 1 is the only road access to Port Fourchon, which services virtually all deep-sea oil operations in the Gulf of Mexico, or about 18 percent of the nation's oil supply. Flooding of this road effectively closes this port. Because of Port Fourchon's significance to the oil industry at the national, state, and local levels, the U.S. Department of Homeland Security, in July 2011, estimated that a closure of 90 days could reduce the national gross domestic product by about $7.8 billion.[23] Figure 4 shows Louisiana State Highway 1 leading to Port Fourchon.

Source: NOAA. GAO-14-504T.

Figure 4. Louisiana State Highway 1 Leading to Port Fourchon.

We found in April 2013, that infrastructure decision makers have not systematically incorporated potential climate change impacts in planning for roads, bridges, and wastewater management systems because, among other factors, they face challenges identifying and obtaining available climate change information best suited for their projects.[24] Even when good scientific information is available, it may not be in the actionable, practical form needed for decision makers to use in planning and designing infrastructure. Such decision makers work with traditional engineering processes, which often require very specific and discrete information. Moreover, local decision makers—who, in this case, specialize in infrastructure planning, not climate science—need assistance from experts who can help them translate available climate change information into something that is locally relevant. In our site visits to several locations where decision makers overcame these challenges—including Louisiana State Highway 1—state and local officials emphasized the role that the federal government could play in helping to increase local resilience.

Any effective adaptation strategy must recognize that state and local governments are on the front lines in both responding to immediate weather-related disasters and in preparing for the potential longer-term impacts associated with climate change. We reported in October 2009, that insufficient site-specific data—such as local temperature and precipitation projections—complicate state and local decisions to justify the current costs of adaptation efforts for potentially less certain future benefits.[25] We recommended that the appropriate entities within the Executive Office of the President develop a strategic plan for adaptation that, among other things, identifies mechanisms to increase the capacity of federal, state, and local agencies to incorporate information about current and potential climate change impacts into government decision making. USGCRP's April 2012 strategic plan for climate change science recognizes this need, by identifying enhanced information management and sharing as a key objective.[26] According to this plan, According to this plan, USGCRP is pursuing the development of a global change information system to leverage existing climate-related tools, services, and portals from federal agencies.

In our April 2013 report, we concluded that the federal government could help state and local efforts to increase their resilience by (1) improving access to and use of available climate-related information, (2) providing officials with improved access to technical assistance, and (3) helping officials consider climate change in their planning processes.[27]

As a result, we recommended, among other things, that the Executive Director of USGCRP or other federal entity designated by the Executive Office of the President work with relevant agencies to identify for decision makers the "best available" climate-related information for infrastructure planning and update this information over time, and to clarify sources of local assistance for incorporating climate-related information and analysis into infrastructure planning, and communicate how such assistance will be provided over time.

These entities have not directly responded to our recommendations, but the President's June 2013 Climate Action Plan and November 2013 Executive Order 13653 drew attention to the need for improved technical assistance.[28] For example, the Executive Order directs numerous federal agencies, supported by USGCRP, to work together to develop and provide authoritative, easily accessible, usable, and timely data, information, and decision-support tools on climate preparedness and resilience. In addition, on July 16, 2014, the President announced a series of actions to help state, local, and tribal leaders prepare their communities for the impacts of climate change by developing more resilient infrastructure and rebuilding existing infrastructure stronger and smarter.[29]

We have work under way assessing the strengths and limitations of governmentwide options to meet the climate-related information needs of federal, state, local, and private sector decision makers. We also have work under way exploring, among other things, the risks extreme weather events and climate change pose to public health, agriculture, public transit systems, and federal insurance programs. This work may help identify other steps the federal government could take to limit its fiscal exposure and make our communities more resilient to extreme weather events.

Chairman Murray, Ranking Member Sessions, and Members of the Committee, this concludes my prepared statement. I would be pleased to answer any questions you have at this time.

End Notes

[1] Our past work identified a variety of fiscal exposures—responsibilities, programs, and activities that explicitly or implicitly expose the federal government to future spending. Fiscal exposures vary widely as to source, extent of the government's legal commitment, and magnitude. Further, some of these factors may change over time. For example, the government's response to an event or series of events can strengthen expectations that the government will respond in the same way to similar events in the future. For additional

information, see Fiscal Exposures: Improving Cost Recognition in the Federal Budget, GAO-14-28 (Washington, D.C.: Oct. 29, 2013).

[2] Melillo, Jerry M., Terese (T.C.) Richmond, and Gary W. Yohe, Eds., 2014: Climate Change Impacts in the United States: The Third National Climate Assessment. U.S. Global Change Research Program (Washington D.C.: May 2014).

[3] U.S. National Academy of Sciences and The Royal Society, Climate Change: Evidence and Causes (Washington, D.C.: Feb 27, 2014).

[4] Congress temporarily increased the borrowing authority for the National Flood Insurance Program by $9.7 billion and provided about $50 billion in appropriated funds for expenses related to the consequences of Superstorm Sandy.

[5] GAO, High-Risk Series: An Update, GAO-13-283, February 2013. Every 2 years at the start of a new Congress, GAO calls attention to agencies and program areas that are high-risk due to their vulnerabilities to fraud, waste, abuse, and mismanagement, or are most in need of transformation.

[6] The National Academies, Committee on Increasing National Resilience to Hazards and Disasters; Committee on Science, Engineering, and Public Policy; Disaster Resilience: A National Imperative (Washington, D.C., 2012).

[7] GAO, Climate Change: Future Federal Adaptation Efforts Could Better Support Local Infrastructure Decision Makers, GAO-13-242 (Washington, D.C.: Apr 12, 2013).

[8] For example, visit http://www.whitehouse.gov/administration/eop/ceq/ initiatives/resilience to access the Climate Change Resilience website maintained by the Council on Environmental Quality (CEQ) within the Executive Office of the President.

[9] See, for example, NRC, Panel on Strategies and Methods for Climate-Related Decision Support, Committee on the Human Dimensions of Global Change, Informing Decisions in a Changing Climate (Washington, D.C.: 2009).

[10] GAO, Climate Change Adaptation: DOD Can Improve Infrastructure Planning and Processes to Better Account for Potential Impacts, GAO-14-446 (Washington, D.C.: May 30, 2014).

[11] GAO-14-446. Adaptation is defined as adjustments to natural or human systems in response to actual or expected climate change.

[12] GAO-13-242.

[13] GAO, Climate Change: Various Adaptation Efforts Are Under Way at Key Natural Resource Management Agencies, GAO-13-253 (Washington, D.C.: May 31, 2013).

[14] Melillo, Jerry M., Terese (T.C.) Richmond, and Gary W. Yohe, Eds., 2014: Climate Change Impacts in the United States: The Third National Climate Assessment. U.S. Global Change Research Program (Washington D.C.: May 2014).

[15] Visit http://www.gao.gov/key_issues/wildland_fire_management/issue_summary to access a summary of wildland fire management issues and related reports on GAO's Key Issues website. See also Congressional Research Service, Wildfire Management: Federal Funding and Related Statistics, R43077 (March 5, 2014).

[16] GAO-13-283.

[17] Executive Order 13514, Federal Leadership in Environmental, Energy, and Economic Performance (Oct. 5, 2009). Executive Order 13653, Preparing the United States for the Impacts of Climate Change (Nov. 1, 2013).

[18] GAO-14-446.

[19] GAO, Climate Change: Agencies Should Develop Guidance for Addressing the Effects on Federal Land and Water Resources, GAO-07-863 (Washington, D.C.: Aug. 7, 2007).

[20]. GAO-13-253.

[21] Congressional Budget Office, Public Spending on Transportation and Water Infrastructure, Pub. No. 4088 (Washington, D.C.: November 2010).

[22] GAO-13-242.

[23] Department of Homeland Security, National Infrastructure Simulation and Analysis Center, Risk Development and Modeling Branch, Homeland Infrastructure Threat and Risk Analysis Center, Office of Infrastructure Protection, in collaboration with the National Incident Management Systems and Advanced Technologies Institute at the University of Louisiana at Lafayette, Louisiana Highway 1/Port Fourchon Study (July 15, 2011).

[24] GAO-13-242.

[25] GAO, Climate Change Adaptation: Strategic Federal Planning Could Help Government Officials Make More Informed Decisions, GAO-10-113 (Washington, D.C.: Oct. 7, 2009).

[26] USGCRP, National Global Change Research Plan 2012-2021: A Strategic Plan for the U.S. Global Change Research Program (Washington D.C.: April 2012).

[27] GAO-13-242.

[28] More information on the June 2013 Climate Action Plan and Executive Order 13653 can be found at http://www.whitehouse.gov/administration/eop/ceq/initiatives/resilience

[29] Visit http://www.whitehouse.gov/the-press-office/2014/07/16/fact-sheet-taking-action-support-state-local-and-tribal-leaders-they-pre for more information on the resilience efforts announced on July 16, 2014.

In: Fiscal Exposures
Editor: Landon P. Merrill

ISBN: 978-1-63463-589-9

Chapter 3

DISASTER RESILIENCE: ACTIONS ARE UNDERWAY, BUT FEDERAL FISCAL EXPOSURE HIGHLIGHTS THE NEED FOR CONTINUED ATTENTION TO LONGSTANDING CHALLENGES*

Chris Currie

WHY GAO DID THIS STUDY

Multiple factors including increased disaster declarations, climate change effects, and insufficient premiums under the National Flood Insurance Program increase federal fiscal exposure to severe weather events. Managing fiscal exposure from climate change and the National Flood Insurance Program are both on GAO's High Risk list. GAO has previously reported that building resilience to protect against future damage is one strategy to help limit fiscal exposure. However, in prior reports GAO also identified multiple challenges to doing so. Responsibility for actions that enhance resilience rests

* This is an edited, reformatted and augmented version of a report, GAO-14-603T, issued by the U.S. Government Accountability Office, May 14, 2014. This report was originally presented as testimony before the Senate Committee on Homeland Security and Governmental Affairs, Subcommittee on Emergency Management, Intergovernmental Relations and the District of Columbia. Chris Currie is Acting Director, Homeland Security and Justice at the GAO.

largely outside the federal government, so nonfederal entities also play a key role.

This testimony discusses (1) resilience-building challenges GAO has previously identified; (2) federal efforts to facilitate resilience-building as part of Hurricane Sandy recovery; and (3) examples of nonfederal efforts to incentivize resilience building. This testimony is based on previous GAO reports issued from 1998 through 2014 related to hazard mitigation, climate change, flood insurance, and preliminary observations from GAO's ongoing work for this committee on federal resilience efforts related to the Sandy recovery. For the ongoing work, GAO reviewed documents such as the Hurricane Sandy Rebuilding Strategy and a 2012 National Academies study on building resilience. GAO also interviewed officials from FEMA and the Department of Housing and Urban Development (HUD).

What GAO Found

GAO has identified various challenges to resilience building—actions to help prepare and plan for, absorb, recover from, and more successfully adapt to adverse events including those caused by extreme weather. These include challenges for communities in balancing hazard mitigation investments with economic development goals, challenges for individuals in understanding and acting to limit their personal risk, and broad challenges with the clarity of information to inform risk decision making. GAO's work over more than 30 years demonstrates that these are longstanding policy issues, without easy solutions. The Department of Homeland Security's (DHS) May 2013 release of a National Mitigation Framework and establishment of a group to help coordinate interagency and intergovernmental mitigation efforts offers one avenue for leadership on these issues.

In ongoing work on federal resilience efforts in the aftermath of Hurricane Sandy, GAO identified three high-level actions that demonstrated an intensified federal focus on incorporating resilience-building into the recovery.

- The President issued an executive order to coordinate the recovery effort and created a task force that issued 69 recommendations aimed at improving recovery from Sandy and future disasters—including recommendations designed to facilitate resilient rebuilding.
- Congress appropriated about $50 billion in supplemental funds for multiple recovery efforts, including at least five federal programs that

help support resilience-building efforts. One of these, FEMA's Hazard Mitigation Grant Program (HMGP), is the only federal program designed specifically to promote mitigation against future losses in the wake of a disaster; while, another, the Public Transportation Emergency Relief Program made more than $4 billion available for transit resilience projects.

- The Sandy Recovery Improvement Act of 2013 provided additional responsibilities and authorities related to FEMA's mitigation and recovery efforts. In response, FEMA has undertaken efforts to make HMGP easier for states to use—for example by streamlining application procedures. The act also provided additional authorities for FEMA to fund hazard mitigation with other disaster relief funds and required FEMA to provide recommendations for a national strategy on reducing the cost of future disasters to Congress, which FEMA finalized in September 2013.

For the purposes of this statement GAO reviewed studies that discuss resilience building and climate change adaptation and identified examples of efforts at the state and local levels that illustrate a variety of nonfederal initiatives that may drive communities to build resilience. For example, a nonprofit group is creating report cards to assess the resilience of a building to earthquakes, and the group plans to extend these efforts to wind and flood risk. In some localities public-private partnerships have helped promote efforts to buy properties that were at risk from repeat losses.

* * *

Chairman Begich, Ranking Member Paul, and Members of the Subcommittee:

I appreciate the opportunity to testify before you today about disaster mitigation and resilience, especially given the $50 billion in federal dollars recently appropriated for recovery from Hurricane Sandy.[1]

The term resilience refers to the ability to prepare and plan for, absorb, recover from, and more successfully adapt to actual or potential adverse events. Hazard mitigation and climate adaptation are strategies to promote resilience to extreme weather events, among other things. The term mitigation, in this context, describes the capabilities necessary to reduce loss of life and property by lessening the impact of disasters; while, climate change adaptation is specific to such adjustments made in response to actual or expected climate change. These resilience-building strategies include efforts to protect critical infrastructure and reduce specific vulnerabilities—by for example, increasing the capacity of storm water systems and raising river or coastal dikes.

As we reported in 2012, from fiscal years 2004 through 2011, the Federal Emergency Management Agency (FEMA) obligated over $80 billion in federal assistance for disasters, and the growing number of major disaster declarations had contributed to increasing federal disaster assistance expenditures.[2] Moreover, the United States Global Change Research Program has reported that the impacts and costliness of weather disasters—resulting from floods, drought, and other events such as hurricanes—will increase in significance as what are considered "rare" events become more common and intense due to climate change.[3] In addition, less acute effects of changes in the climate, such as sea level rise, could also result in significant long-term effects on people and property. In 2013, we added managing fiscal exposure due to climate change to our High Risk list, in part, because of concerns about these increasing costs.[4]

We also designated the National Flood Insurance Program—a key component of the federal government's efforts to limit the financial impact of floods—as a high risk area and included it on our High Risk list in March 2006.[5] The program faces challenges with long-term sustainability—as of December 2013, FEMA's debt from flood insurance payments totaled about $24 billion—and FEMA had not repaid any principal on the loan since 2010—which compounds fiscal exposure arising from severe weather events.

We and others have recommended building resilience—by taking actions to mitigate vulnerabilities to the effects of severe weather and to adapt to effects of climate change—as one strategy to help to limit the nation's fiscal exposure.[6] However, we have previously identified a variety of challenges associated with such resilience-building efforts.

In October 2012, Hurricane Sandy devastated the Eastern seaboard and resulted in tens of billions of dollars damage from the Mid-Atlantic to the Northeast. At the same time, an executive order and legislation in the wake of the devastation signaled an increased focus from both the President and Congress on building resilience into recovery efforts.

We currently have ongoing work for this committee evaluating select federal efforts to facilitate resilience planning and activities as part of the Sandy recovery effort, which we plan to issue later this year. My statement today is based on previously published and ongoing work and it discusses select (1) resilience-building challenges we have previously identified; (2)

federal efforts to facilitate resilience-building as part of the Sandy recovery; and (3) examples of nonfederal efforts to incentivize resilience building.

This statement is based on reports we issued from January 1998 to August 2007 on hazard mitigation and resilience-building activities and ongoing work for this committee evaluating federal efforts to facilitate resilience planning and activities as part of the Sandy recovery efforts. Specifically, to describe resilience building challenges we have previously identified, we consulted our prior reports and testimonies (see Related GAO Products at the end of this statement). For our prior work, among other things, we reviewed key federal documents and efforts such as previous congressional reports and publications from the federal agencies involved in mitigation activities, analyzed information collected from relevant agencies and officials, and visited locations with comprehensive mitigation programs. Further details on the scope and methodology of our previously issued reports are available within each of the published products. For our ongoing work on federal mitigation efforts, we reviewed documents such as the Hurricane Sandy Rebuilding Strategy and FEMA's report on recommendations for a national strategy to reduce the costs of future disasters, and studies on nonfederal resilience-building efforts, and we interviewed federal officials at FEMA and the Department of Housing and Urban Development (HUD).[7] We shared a copy of the new information in this statement with Department of Homeland Security (DHS) officials.

The work upon which this testimony is based was and is being conducted in accordance with generally accepted government auditing standards. Those standards require that we plan and perform the audit to obtain sufficient, appropriate evidence to provide a reasonable basis for our findings and conclusions based on our audit objectives. We believe that the evidence obtained provides a reasonable basis for our findings and conclusions based on our audit objectives.

LONGSTANDING CHALLENGES INHIBIT EFFORTS TO PROMOTE RESILIENCE

Challenges we identified with disaster resilience as long ago as 1980 have persisted and were reflected in our work on disaster mitigation in 2007, as well as recent studies such as a 2012 National Academies National Research Council (NRC) study on disaster resilience.[8]

State and Local Governments May Have Concerns about Competing Priorities for Economic Development and Resilience Building

We testified in January 1998 that, for a number of reasons, state and local governments may be reluctant to invest in resilience-building efforts.[9] For example, leaders may be concerned that hazard mitigation activities will detract from economic development goals and may perceive that mitigation is costly and involves solutions that are overly technical and complex.

In our work on hazard mitigation issued in August 2007, we found that these issues persisted. We reported that hazard mitigation goals and local economic interests often conflict, and the resulting tension can often have a profound effect on mitigation efforts.[10] For example, we reported that community goals such as building housing and promoting economic development may be higher priorities than formulating mitigation regulations that may include restrictive development regulations and more stringent building codes. In particular, local government officials we contacted as part of that work commented that developers often want to increase growth in hazard-prone areas (e.g., along the coast or in floodplains) to support economic development. These areas are often desirable for residences and businesses, and such development increases local tax revenues but is generally in conflict with mitigation goals.

In 2012, the National Academies National Research Council (NRC) issued a report on disaster resilience, noting that understanding, managing, and reducing disaster risks provide a foundation for building resilience to disasters.[11] Risk management—both personal and collective—is important in the resilience context because the perceptions of and choices about risk shape how individuals, groups, and public- and private-sector organizations behave, how they respond during and after a disaster event, and how they plan for future disasters. However, the National Academies report described a variety of challenges that affect risk management. As with our 1998 and 2007 work, one of the key challenges the NRC reported for state and local governments was reluctance to limit economic development with resilience measures.

Individuals May Lack Incentives and Understanding of Risk When Deciding Whether to Invest in Resilience-Building Efforts

We testified in January 1998 that individuals may also lack incentives to take resilience-building measures.[12] We noted that increasing the awareness of the hazards associated with living in a certain area or previous experience with disasters do not necessarily persuade individuals to take preventive measures against future disasters. Residents of hazard-prone areas tend to treat the possibility of a disaster's occurrence as sufficiently low to permit them to ignore the consequences.

We have also reported that the availability of federal assistance may inhibit actions to mitigate disaster losses. As long ago as 1980, we reported that individuals may not act to protect themselves from the effects of severe weather if they believe the federal government will eventually help pay for their losses.[13] The 1993 National Performance Review also found that the availability of post-disaster federal funds may reduce incentives for mitigation.[14] Moreover, FEMA's 1993 review of the National Earthquake Hazards Reduction Program concluded that at the state level there is "the expectation that federal disaster assistance will address the problem after the event.[15] Concerns about individuals' ability to appropriately evaluate risk and take action to protect themselves continued in our August 2007 work when we reported that individuals often have a misperception that natural hazard events will not occur in their community and are not interested in learning of the likelihood of an event occurring.[16] Likewise, the 2012 NRC report on disaster resilience identified the key risk management challenge for homeowners and businesses in hazard-prone areas is the fact that they may be unaware of or underestimate the hazards that they face.[17]

Information Required to Support Risk Decision Making is Imprecise, Incomplete, and Complex

In January 1998, we described three sets of issues that complicate assessing the cost-effectiveness of actions to build resilience.[18] At the same time, we testified that a lack of comprehensive, reliable data to make decisions about cost-benefit tradeoffs may also inhibit local governments from deciding to invest in hazard mitigation activities. First, we noted that by definition, natural hazard mitigation reduces the loss of life and property below the levels that could be expected without mitigation, but it is impossible to measure what loss would have been incurred without mitigation. Second, the dispersion of mitigation funds and responsibilities across various agencies makes it difficult to determine the collective benefit of federal efforts. Finally, we noted that federal savings depend on the frequency of future disasters and the extent to which the federal government will bear the resulting losses, which is unknown.

Moreover, in 2007 we reported that limited public awareness may also be a result of the complexity of the information that is needed for individuals to understand their hazard risks.[19] We concluded that for local decision makers to develop mitigation strategies for their communities they need appropriate and easily understandable information about the probability of natural hazards and that efforts to improve public awareness and education are long-term and require sustained effort. Similarly, in our February 2014 testimony on limiting fiscal exposure from and increasing resilience to climate change, we noted that local decision makers need expert assistance translating climate change information into something that is locally relevant. The 2012 NRC study identified understanding how to share scientific information with broad audiences as one of the key challenges for resilience researchers.

The challenges we identified in prior work—competing priorities for state and local governments, imperfect individual risk decision making, and imprecise, incomplete, and complex information about both risk and benefits—are difficult issues that are likely to persist. These issues are longstanding and difficult policy issues. Indeed, the increasing number of federal disaster declarations and the growing role of the federal government in funding post disaster relief and recovery efforts may serve to exacerbate some of the inherent challenges. We are encouraged that DHS finalized the National Mitigation Framework in 2013 to coordinate interagency and intergovernmental efforts and that the framework established a Mitigation Framework Leadership Group to coordinate mitigation efforts of relevant local, state, tribal, and federal organizations. The framework and the group create an avenue for interagency and intergovernmental leadership to pursue solutions to these difficult policy issues. As part of our ongoing work, we plan to evaluate the status of the Mitigation Framework Leadership Group and the actions taken to date to apply the National Mitigation Framework in the context of recovery from Hurricane Sandy.

FEDERAL RESPONSE TO HURRICANE SANDY DEMONSTRATED INCREASED FOCUS ON MITIGATION AND RESILIENCE-BUILDING

In ongoing work on federal resilience efforts in the aftermath of Hurricane Sandy, we identified three high-level actions that demonstrated an intensified federal focus on incorporating resilience-building into the recovery.

The President's Executive Order on Sandy Rebuilding Charged Federal Agencies with Facilitating Resilience

In the wake of Hurricane Sandy, President Obama signed Executive Order 13632 on December 7, 2012.[20] The Executive Order created the Hurricane Sandy Rebuilding Task Force, chaired by the HUD Secretary and consisting of more than 23 federal agencies and offices. Among other things, the executive order charged the task force to work with partners in the affected region to understand existing and future risks and vulnerabilities from extreme weather events; identify resources and authorities that strengthen community and regional resilience during recovery; and plan for the rebuilding of critical infrastructure in a manner that increases community and regional resilience. The order also charged the task force with helping to identify and remove obstacles to resilient rebuilding and promoting long-term sustainability of communities and ecosystems.

In August 2013, the Sandy Rebuilding Task Force issued the Hurricane Sandy Rebuilding Strategy, which contained 69 recommendations to various federal agencies and their nonfederal partners aimed at improving recovery from both Hurricane Sandy and future disasters. Among these 69 recommendations are many that take into account the President's charge to facilitate planning and actions to build resilience in the Sandy-affected region. Introducing the strategy, the task force chair acknowledged how critical it was that efforts to rebuild for the future make communities more resilient to emerging challenges such as rising sea levels, extreme heat, and more frequent and intense storms.

The task force report notes that many of the recommendations have been adopted and describes actions underway to implement them as part of the Hurricane Sandy recovery effort. Key examples of long-term resilient rebuilding initiatives to address future risks to extreme weather events include the Rebuild by Design effort and the New York Rising Community Reconstruction Program. In June 2013, HUD and its partners launched the Rebuild by Design competition to challenge communities to develop solutions to address structural and environmental vulnerabilities exposed by Hurricane Sandy. Of the 148 applicants, HUD selected 10 to move forward.[21] The selected teams then worked with local stakeholders to tailor their projects to the communities and hosted over 50 community workshops to educate the communities on their proposals and the theme of resilience. On April 3, 2014, the final proposals were exhibited and evaluated by an expert jury. Winning design solutions may be awarded disaster recovery grants from HUD and other public and private partners. Some resilience aspects of the designs include elevating streets and adding breakwater systems.

The New York Rising Community Reconstruction Program is another mitigation program that provides over $650 million for additional rebuilding and revitalization planning and implementation assistance to Sandy-affected communities. As of May 2014, six regions of New York composed of 102 localities and 50 New York Rising communities created plans that assessed storm damage and current risk, identified community needs and opportunities, and developed recovery and resilient strategies. Each locality is eligible for $3 million to $25 million from HUD and other public and private partners. According to the State of New York, as of May 2014, multiple projects had been awarded funding.

As part of our ongoing work on resilience-building as part of the Hurricane Sandy recovery, we are identifying recommendations from the task force report that particularly support resilient rebuilding and assessing the actions taken to date to implement them. We plan to issue a report on these issues later this year.

Congress Appropriated Funds to Key Federal Programs that Can Help Support Resilient Rebuilding

In January 2013, Congress passed and the President signed the Disaster Relief Appropriations Act, 2013 (Sandy Supplemental), which appropriated about $50 billion in funding to support recovery.[22] The Sandy Supplemental appropriated funds—primarily for programs and activities associated with recovery from Hurricane Sandy— to nineteen federal agencies. Among the nineteen agencies, four—DHS, HUD, the Department of Transportation (DOT), and U.S. Army Corps of Engineers (USACE)—received amounts that represent over 92 percent of the total with appropriations ranging from $5 billion to $15 billion.[23] These four agencies administer five programs that play a key role in helping to promote resilience-building as part of recovery: (1) FEMA's Hazard Mitigation Grant Program (HMGP), (2) FEMA's Public Assistance Program (PA), (3) HUD's Community Development Block Grant-Disaster Recovery (CDBG-DR) Program, (4) DOT's Federal Transit Administration (FTA) Public Transportation Emergency Relief Program, and (5) USACE's Flood Risk Management Program. See table 1 for a description of these programs and how they help to support resilience-building efforts.

Table 1. Key Federal Programs Funded by Sandy Supplemental that Support Resilience Building

Agency	Program	Who Can Apply	How It Supports Resilience-Building	How It Is Used in Sandy Recovery
Federal Emergency Management Agency (FEMA)	Hazard Mitigation Grant Program	state, tribal, and local governments	the only federal program explicitly designed to improve resilience to future disasters during recovery funds a wide range of projects, including purchasing properties in flood-prone areas, adding shutters to windows to prevent future damage from hurricane winds and rains, or rebuilding culverts in drainage ditches to prevent future flooding damage	FEMA estimates that the program will provide about $349 million from inception through fiscal year 2014 for mitigation activities.

Table 1. (Continued)

Agency	Program	Who Can Apply	How It Supports Resilience-Building	How It Is Used in Sandy Recovery
FEMA	Public Assistance	state, tribal, and local governments and some nonprofit organizations	may fund measures to reduce future risks in conjunction with repair of disaster damaged facilities if cost-effectiveness can be demonstrated	In total, FEMA estimates that it will spend $8.5 billion on public assistance for Sandy recovery by the end of fiscal year 2014, some of which can be used to reduce future risks
Housing and Urban Development (HUD)	Community Development Block Grant—Disaster Recovery	states and local governments—not less than 50 percent of funds must benefit low and moderate income persons, but grantees may seek to reduce the overall benefit requirement below the 50 percent with justification	designed to address needs not met by other disaster recovery programs, which can include resilience-building projects	In conjunction with its leadership on the Sandy Rebuilding Task Force, HUD linked key resilience-building initiatives to the grant program. For example, these funds can be awarded to Rebuild by Design and New York Rising communities to carry out those projects.
Federal Transit Administration	Public Transportation Emergency Relief Program	transit authorities	can fund transit resilience projects	$4.3 billion has been made available for resilience projects
U.S. Army Corps of Engineers (USACE)	National Flood Risk Management Program	not a grant program	costal and river flood prevention	USACE is using a portion of its $5 billion in Sandy Supplemental funds—about $1 billion—to reduce future flood risk in

Agency	Program	Who Can Apply	How It Supports Resilience-Building	How It Is Used in Sandy Recovery
				ways that will support the long term sustainability of the costal ecosystem and communities and reduce the economic costs associated with large-scale flooding.

Source: GAO Analysis of Federal Guidance and Policy.

Legislation to Improve Recovery Activities Also Focuses on Resilient Rebuilding

As part of our ongoing work we plan to focus on efforts within FEMA's HMGP and PA and HUD's CDBG-DR to facilitate and support community and regional resilience efforts as part of recovery from Hurricane Sandy. We are evaluating federal actions, gathering perspectives from key state officials, and studying at least one large-scale PA project that involves resilience-building activates.

The Sandy Recovery Improvement Act of 2013 (SRIA) was enacted as part of the Sandy Supplemental.[24] The law authorizes several significant changes to the way FEMA may deliver federal disaster assistance. FEMA is tracking its implementation of 17 provisions of the act, of which are aimed at mitigating future damage. Specifically:

- *Public Assistance Work Alternative Procedures.* This section authorizes FEMA to implement alternative procedures for administration of the PA program with the aim of providing greater flexibility and less administrative burden by basing grants on fixed estimates. Among the provisions in this section of SRIA is one that would allow use of all or part of the excess grant funds awarded for the repair, restoration, and replacement of damaged facilities for cost effective activities that mitigate the risk of future damage, hardship, or suffering from a major disaster.

- *Changes to HMGP.* SRIA authorized three key changes to HMGP. First, it authorizes FEMA to expedite implementation of the program. FEMA has issued guidance for streamlining the program and is planning actions to continue to refine the changes and measure their effectiveness. Second, SRIA allows FEMA to provide up to 25 percent of the estimated costs for eligible hazard mitigation measures to a state or tribal grantee before eligible costs are incurred. As part of the revised, streamlined HMGP guidance, FEMA has informed states of this provision. Third, SRIA allows FEMA to waive notice and comment rulemaking procedures for HMGP Administration by States and authorizes FEMA to carry out the program as a pilot. FEMA is currently carrying out a pilot program and issued a notice in the Federal Register in March 2014 seeking comments from the public to help inform the development of this new method of program delivery.[25] To develop the program, FEMA is exploring the extent to which its determinations regarding cost-effectiveness, technical feasibility and engineering, and final eligibility and funding can be made at the state level.
- *National Strategy to Reduce Costs on Future Disasters.* SRIA required FEMA to make recommendations for the development of a national strategy to reduce costs on future disasters. In September 2013 FEMA issued the required report, recommending that the following elements be considered in the development of a national strategy: 1) engage in a whole community dialogue and build upon public-private partnerships, 2) enhance data-driven decisions, 3) align incentives promoting disaster cost reduction and resilience, 4) enable resilient recovery, and 5) support disaster risk reduction nationally.[26]

Nonfederal Groups Have a Variety of Initiatives to Help Incentivize Resilience Building

As we have previously reported, most responsibility and authority for resilience activities rests largely outside the federal government; therefore, nonfederal incentives are also a critical piece of the overall strategy to reduce future losses. [27] The federal government, by providing incentives through programs like the five discussed earlier in this statement, can help to promote and facilitate mitigation before and after disasters. However, ultimately, nonfederal entities inside and outside the government make the decisions that lead (or do not lead) to resilience activities. Several examples of mitigation efforts at the state and local levels help illustrate the variety of ways that incentives help drive communities to be more resilient—with a range of activities from shoring up building codes to facilitating buyouts of repetitive loss properties.

As part of our ongoing work, we are reviewing studies about efforts to build resilience to extreme weather events and climate change. For the purposes of this statement, we selected illustrative examples from those studies to describe a range of nonfederal efforts to incentivize mitigation.

The 2012 NRC report discussed earlier in this statement included several examples of earthquake mitigation efforts in California.[28]

- In California, zones of potential landslide, liquefaction, or fault rupture hazard have been mapped by the California Geological Survey as "special study zones" according to provisions in the California AlquistPriolo Earthquake Fault Zoning Act of 1972. If a property is in one of these special study zones, the buyers must sign a form indicating that they have been made aware of this potential hazard and recognize that additional inspections and work may be required if they choose to modify the property in the future.
- The U.S. Resiliency Council, a nonprofit organization based in California, is working on creating building "report cards" to provide technically defensible metrics to evaluate and communicate the resilience of individual buildings. The initial focus is on seismic risk, and officials plan to extend their efforts to creating metrics for resilience to catastrophic wind and flood risk. Transparency and required disclosure of these individual building resilience ratings can benefit building users, owners, and lenders by increasing the value of well designed or properly retrofitted properties.
- The Property Transfer Tax Program in Berkeley, California has provided funds for seismically retrofitting a number of properties in the city. In 1992, voters approved an additional 0.5 percent transfer tax on top of the existing 1 percent tax on all real estate transactions, with the tax paid equally by buyer and seller. This portion of the transfer tax is available for voluntary seismic upgrades to residential property. Residential property owners have up to 1 year to complete the seismic retrofit (or lose the funds). Since many homes sell for $750,000 to $1 million or more in Berkeley, this amounted to $3,750-

5,000 in "free funds" and can cover homeowner upgrades such as brick chimney bracing or anchoring water heaters. This incentive program has an 80 to-90 percent participation rate. Along with other measures, this program has led to more than 60 percent of the residences in Berkeley becoming more resistant to earthquakes.

Similarly, the Columbia Center for Climate Change Law of Columbia Law School issued a report in 2013 that included examples of flood mitigation efforts in North Dakota and Iowa. [29]

- In 1996, 83 percent of the homes in Grand Forks, ND were damaged when the Red River reached 54 feet and topped the city dikes. Using CDBG funding, the City of Grand Forks purchased 802 lots, moved salvageable homes, and destroyed the remainder to create a green space. The city also partnered with a private development company to finance the construction of 180 new homes in an underdeveloped area of Grand Forks to help relocate some of the people who had lost their homes in the flooding and subsequent buy-out program.
- In 1993, the Iowa River flooded, and overtopped existing levees. The US Army Corps of Engineers planned to rebuild and repair the levees—but a working group of state and federal agencies determined that the best solution would be to buy all the homes in the levee district so that it could be statutorily dissolved and the city would no longer have to support the infrastructure in the area. The buyout program developed a novel land-transfer system and engaged government agencies and non-profit organizations to execute it. The non-profit organization's role was instrumental because landowners were hesitant to sell their property to the government, but were comfortable selling it to the non-profit. The non-profit used a formula to set the land price, which contributed to the success of the buyout because purchasers didn't have to negotiate prices with each individual landowner and it removed the incentive for landowners to hold out for a better price.

Chairman Begich, Ranking Member Paul, and members of the subcommittee, this completes my prepared statement. I would be happy to respond to any questions you may have at this time.

GAO Related Products

Extreme Weather Events: Limiting Federal Fiscal Exposure and Increasing the Nation's Resilience. GAO-14-364T. Washington, D.C.: February 12, 2014.

High-Risk Series: An Update. GAO-13-283. Washington, D.C.: February 14, 2013.

Federal Disaster Assistance: Improved Criteria Needed to Assess a Jurisdiction's Capability to Respond and Recover on Its Own. GAO-12-838. Washington, D.C.: September 12, 2012.

Natural Hazard Mitigation: Various Mitigation Efforts Exist, but Federal Efforts Do Not Provide a Comprehensive Strategic Framework. GAO-07-403. Washington, D.C.: August 22, 2007.

High Risk Series: GAO's High-Risk Program. GAO-06-497T. Washington, D.C.: March 15, 2006.

Disaster Assistance: Information on the Cost-Effectiveness of Hazard Mitigation Projects. GAO/T-RCED-99-106. Washington, D.C.: March 4, 1999.

Disaster Assistance: Information on Federal Disaster Mitigation Efforts. GAO/T-RCED-98-67. Washington, D.C.: January 28, 1998.

Disaster Assistance: Information on Expenditures and Proposals to Improve Effectiveness and Reduce Future Costs. GAO/T-RCED-95-140. Washington, D.C.: March 16, 1995.

Federal Disaster Assistance: What Should the Policy Be? PAD-80-39. Washington, D.C.: June 16, 1980.

End Notes

[1] The Disaster Relief Appropriations Act of 2013 (appropriated approximately $50 billion for disaster recovery Pub. L. No. 113-2, div. A, 127 Stat. 4 (2013). The majority of appropriation accounts that received funding were subject to a reduction of 5.0 percent of their budgetary resources.

[2] GAO, Federal Disaster Assistance: Improved Criteria Needed to Assess a Jurisdiction's Capability to Respond and Recover on Its Own, GAO-12-838 (Washington, D.C.: Sep. 12, 2012).

[3] Thomas R. Karl, Jerry M. Melillo, and Thomas C. Peterson, eds. Global Climate Change Impacts in the United States, (Cambridge University Press: 2009) and Melillo, Jerry M., Terese (T.C.) Richmond, and Gary W. Yohe, eds. Climate Change Impacts in the United States: The Third National Climate Assessment. U.S. Global Change Research Program (U.S. Government Printing Office: 2014).

[4] GAO, High-Risk Series: An Update, GAO-13-283 (Washington, D.C.: Feb. 14, 2013).

[5] GAO's High Risk Program, GAO-06-497T (Washington, D.C.: Mar. 15, 2006).

[6] The term fiscal exposure refers to the responsibilities, programs, and activities that may either legally commit the federal government to future spending or create the expectation for future spending. See GAO Fiscal Exposures: Improving Cost Recognition in the Federal Budget, GAO-14-28 (Washington, D.C.: Oct. 29, 2013).

[7] Specifically, we reviewed a 2012 study by the National Academies National Resource Council and a 2013 study by the Columbia Center for Climate Change and selected examples to demonstrate a range of nonfederal efforts to incentivize resilience building.

[8] National Research Council. Disaster Resilience: A National Imperative. Washington, DC: The National Academies Press, 2012.

[9] Disaster Assistance: Information on Federal Disaster Mitigation Efforts (GAO/T-RCED-98-67, Jan. 28, 1998).

[10] GAO, Natural Hazard Mitigation: Various Mitigation Efforts Exist, but Federal Efforts Do Not Provide a Comprehensive Strategic Framework (GAO-07-403, Aug 22, 2007). We recommended that the Administrator of FEMA, in consultation with other appropriate federal agencies, develop and maintain a national comprehensive strategic framework for mitigation. In 2013, DHS published the National Mitigation Framework to provide the strategic framework we recommended.

[11] National Research Council. Disaster Resilience: A National Imperative. Washington, DC: The National Academies Press, 2012.

[12] GAO/T-RCED-98-67.

[13] Federal Disaster Assistance: What Should The Policy Be? (PAD-80-39, June 16, 1980).

[14] Creating a Government That Works Better and Costs Less: Federal Emergency Management Agency, National Performance Review (Washington, D.C.: GPO, 1993).

[15] Improving Earthquake Mitigation, FEMA, report to the Congress as required under Pub. L. No. 101-614, § 14(b), 104 Stat. 3231, 3242 (1993), p. 15.

[16] GAO-07-403.

[17] National Research Council. Disaster Resilience: A National Imperative. Washington, DC: The National Academies Press, 2012.

[18] GAO/T-RCED-98-67.

[19] GAO-07-403.

[20] Exec. Order No. 13,632, 77 Fed. Reg. 74,341 (Dec. 14, 2012).

[21] The 10 selected design opportunities applied the Infrastructure Resilience Guidelines set forth in the Sandy Task Force report. The purpose of the guidelines is to outline standards to help govern federal funding for Sandy-related infrastructure investments and promote regional resilience. All federal, state, and local projects must adhere to the seven guidelines to receive federal funding. The guidelines require that all projects have: comprehensive analysis, transparent and inclusive decision processes, regional resilience, long-term efficacy and fiscal sustainability, environmentally sustainable and innovative solutions, targeted financial incentives, and adherence to resilience performance standards.

[22] Pub. L. No. 113-2, 127 Stat. 4 (2013).

[23] The amounts received by these four federal agencies reflect the adjustment for sequester.

[24] Pub. L. No. 113-2, Div. B, 127 Stat. 4, 39 (2013).

[25] 79 Fed. Reg. 13,970 (Mar. 12, 2014).

[26] National Strategy Recommendations: Future Disaster Preparedness, Federal Emergency Management Agency (FEMA) Washington, D.C., September 2013.

[27] GAO/T-RCED-98-67 and GAO-07-403.

[28] National Research Council. Disaster Resilience: A National Imperative. Washington, DC: The National Academies Press, 2012.

[29] Managed Coastal Retreat: A Handbook of Tools, Case Studies, and Lessons Learned, Columbia Center for Climate Change Law, October 2013 New York, NY.

In: Fiscal Exposures
Editor: Landon P. Merrill
ISBN: 978-1-63463-589-9

Chapter 4

EXTREME WEATHER EVENTS: LIMITING FEDERAL FISCAL EXPOSURE AND INCREASING THE NATION'S RESILIENCE*

Mark Gaffigan

WHY GAO DID THIS STUDY

According to the United States Global Change Research Program, the costs and impacts of weather disasters resulting from floods, drought, and other events are expected to increase in significance as previously "rare" events become more common and intense. These impacts pose financial risks to the federal government. While it is not possible to link any individual weather event to climate change, these events provide insight into the potential climate-related vulnerabilities the United States faces.

GAO focuses particular attention on government operations it identifies as posing a "high risk" to the American taxpayer and, in February 2013, added to its High Risk List the area *Limiting the Federal Government's Fiscal Exposure by Better Managing Climate Change Risks*. GAO's past work identified a variety of fiscal exposures—responsibilities, programs, and

* This is an edited, reformatted and augmented version of a report, GAO-14-364T, issued by the U.S. Government Accountability Office, February 12, 2014. This report was originally presented as testimony before the Senate Committee on Homeland Security and Governmental Affairs. Mark Gaffigan is Managing Director, Natural Resources and Environment at the GAO.

activities that may either legally commit the federal government to future spending or create the expectation for future spending in response to extreme weather events. This testimony is based on reports GAO issued from March 2007 to November 2013 that address these issues.

GAO is not making new recommendations but made numerous recommendations in prior reports on these topics, which are in varying states of implementation by the Executive Office of the President and relevant federal agencies

What GAO Found

The federal government has opportunities to limit its exposure and increase the nation's resilience to extreme weather events. Since 1980, the U.S. has experienced 151 weather disasters with damages exceeding 1 billion dollars each. This testimony focuses on 4 areas where the government could limit its fiscal exposure.

- *Property and crop insurance.* The financial risks from two federal insurance programs—the National Flood Insurance Program administered by the Federal Emergency Management Agency (FEMA) and the Federal Crop Insurance Corporation (FCIC)—create a significant fiscal exposure. In 2012, the NFIP had property coverage of over $1.2 trillion and the FCIC had crop coverage of almost $120 billion. As of December 2013, FEMA's debt from flood insurance payments totaled about $24 billion. For various reasons, FCIC's costs more than doubled from $3.4 billion in fiscal year 2001 to $7.6 billion in fiscal year 2012. In 2007, GAO found that the agencies responsible for these programs needed to develop information on their long-term exposure to climate change. The Biggert-Waters Flood Insurance Reform Act of 2012 requires FEMA to use information on future changes in sea levels and other factors in updating flood maps used to set insurance rates. Private insurers are also studying how to include climate change in rate setting. GAO is currently examining the extent to which private and federal insurance programs address risks from climate change.
- *Disaster aid.* The federal government does not fully budget for recovery activities after major disasters, thus creating a large fiscal exposure. GAO reported in 2012 that disaster declarations have

increased to a record 98 in fiscal year 2011 compared with 65 in 2004. Over that period, FEMA obligated over $80 billion for disaster aid. GAO's past work recommended that FEMA address the federal fiscal exposure from disaster assistance.

- *Owner and operator of infrastructure*. The federal government owns and operates hundreds of thousands of facilities that a changing climate could affect. For example, in its 2010 Quadrennial Defense Review, the Department of Defense (DOD) recognized the risk to its facilities posed by climate change, noting that the department must assess the potential impacts and adapt. GAO plans to report later this year on DOD's management of climate change risks at over 500,000 defense facilities.
- *Provider of technical assistance to state and local governments*. The federal government invests billions of dollars annually in infrastructure projects that state and local governments prioritize, such as roads and bridges. Total public spending on transportation and water infrastructure exceeds $300 billion annually, with about 25 percent coming from the federal government and the rest from state and local governments. GAO's April 2013 report on infrastructure adaptation concluded that the federal government could help state and local efforts to increase their resilience by (1) improving access to and use of available climate-related information, (2) providing officials with improved access to local assistance, and (3) helping officials consider climate change in their planning processes.

* * *

Chairman Carper, Ranking Member Coburn, and Members of the Committee:

Thank you for inviting me to discuss our work on opportunities for the federal government to reduce the fiscal exposure and financial risks posed by extreme weather events.[1] According to the United States Global Change Research Program (USGCRP), the impacts and costliness of weather disasters—resulting from floods, drought, and other events such as tropical cyclones—are expected to increase in significance as previously "rare" events become more common and intense due to anticipated changes in the global climate system.[2] Typically, climate change is described as average annual changes in temperature or precipitation, and is associated with shifts in the frequency and severity of extreme weather that can impose substantial costs on society. The 151 weather disasters since 1980 with overall damages exceeding $1 billion each illustrate these vulnerabilities.[3] While it is not possible to link any individual weather event to climate change, these events provide insight into the potential climate-related vulnerabilities the United States faces.

Federal, state, and local policymakers increasingly view adaptation—adjustments to natural or human systems in response to actual or expected climate change—as a risk-management strategy to protect vulnerable sectors and communities that could be affected by extreme weather events and changes in the climate. For example, adaptation measures may include raising river or coastal dikes to protect infrastructure from sea level rise, building higher bridges, and increasing the capacity of storm water systems. As stated in a 2010 National Research Council (NRC) report, even though uncertainties exist regarding the exact nature and magnitude of impacts, mobilizing now to increase the nation's resilience can be an insurance policy against climate change risks.[4]

My testimony today is based on reports we issued from March 2007 to November 2013. We conducted work for these reports in accordance with generally accepted government auditing standards. Our issued reports have detailed information about our scope and methodology.

Limiting Federal Fiscal Exposure and Financial Risks from Extreme Weather Events by Increasing the Nation's Resilience

Among other impacts, climate change could threaten coastal areas with rising sea levels, alter agricultural productivity, and increase the intensity and frequency of severe weather events such as floods, drought, and hurricanes that have cost the nation tens of billions of dollars in damages over the past decade. For example, Congress provided around $60 billion in budget authority for disaster assistance after Superstorm Sandy.[5]

These impacts pose significant financial risks, but the federal government is not well positioned to address this fiscal exposure, partly because of the complex nature of the issue. Given these challenges and the nation's fiscal condition, in February 2013, we added *Limiting the Federal Government's Fiscal Exposure by Better Managing Climate Change Risks* to our list of high-risk areas.[6]

Federal Government as Insurer of Property and Crops

Climate-related impacts will result in increased fiscal exposures for the federal government from many areas, including, but not limited to its role as (1) the insurer of property and crops vulnerable to climate impacts, (2) the provider of aid in response to disasters, (3) the owner or operator of extensive infrastructure such as defense facilities and federal property vulnerable to climate impacts, and (4) the provider of data and technical assistance to state and local governments responsible for managing the impacts of climate change on their activities.

The financial risks from two important federal insurance programs—the National Flood Insurance Program (NFIP) administered by the Federal Emergency Management Agency (FEMA) and the Federal Crop Insurance Corporation (FCIC) administered by the United States Department of Agriculture (USDA)—create a significant fiscal exposure. In 2012, the NFIP had property coverage of over $1.2 trillion and the FCIC had crop coverage of almost $120 billion. NFIP has been on our High Risk List since March 2006 because of concerns about its long-term financial solvency and related operational issues. While Congress and FEMA intended to finance NFIP with premiums collected from policyholders and not with tax dollars, the program was, by design, not intended to pay for itself. As of December 2013, FEMA's debt from flood insurance payments totaled about $24 billion—up from $17.8 billion before Superstorm Sandy—and FEMA had not repaid any principal on the loan since 2010.[7] Further, the federal government's crop insurance costs have increased in recent years for a variety of reasons, more than doubling from $3.4 billion in fiscal year 2001 to $7.6 billion in fiscal year 2012.[8]

In March 2007, we reported that both of these programs' exposure to weather-related losses had grown substantially, and that FEMA and USDA had done little to develop the information necessary to understand their long-term exposure resulting from climate change.[9] We recommended that the Secretaries of Agriculture and Homeland Security analyze the potential long-term fiscal implications of climate change on federal insurance programs and report their findings to Congress. The agencies agreed with the recommendation and contracted with experts to study their programs' long-term exposure from climate change. Both agencies have incorporated the findings of the reports into their climate change adaptation plans—as directed by instructions and guidance implementing Executive Order 13514 on Federal Leadership in Environmental, Energy, and Economic Performance.

We are currently examining how these programs account for climate change in their activities.

In addition, we have previously reported on external factors that complicate the administration of NFIP and affect its financial stability.[10] In June 2011, we reported that FEMA had not been authorized to account for long-term erosion when updating flood maps used to set premium rates for NFIP, increasing the likelihood that premiums would not cover future losses. We therefore suggested that Congress consider authorizing NFIP to account for long-term erosion in its flood maps.[11] Subsequently, Congress passed the Biggert-Waters Flood Insurance Reform Act of 2012 (Biggert-Waters Act), which requires FEMA to use information on topography, coastal erosion areas, changing lake levels, future changes in sea levels, and intensity of hurricanes in updating its flood maps.[12]

The Biggert-Waters Act also reauthorized NFIP through 2017 and made other significant changes to the program, including removing subsidized premium rates for certain properties, eliminating the grandfathering of prior premium rates when a property is remapped, and requiring FEMA to create a reserve fund. While these changes may help put NFIP on a path to financial solvency, their ultimate effect is not yet known. In addition, the program faces challenges in making the changes. For example, implementation of certain changes was delayed by provisions in the Consolidated Appropriations Act of 2014, and S. 1926, which passed the Senate on January 30, 2014, would delay the implementation of certain rate increases contained in the Biggert-Waters Act. As we have previously reported, such delays to rate increases may help address affordability concerns, but they would likely continue to increase NFIP's long-term burden on taxpayers.[13]

Federal Government As Provider of Disaster Aid

In the event of a major disaster, federal funding for response and recovery comes from the Disaster Relief Fund managed by FEMA, and disaster aid programs of other participating federal agencies.[14] The federal government does not fully budget for these costs, thus creating a large fiscal exposure. We reported, in September 2012, that disaster declarations have increased over recent decades to a record of 98 in fiscal year 2011 compared with 65 in 2004.[15] Over that period, FEMA obligated over $80 billion in federal assistance for disasters. We also found that FEMA has had difficulty implementing long-standing plans to assess national preparedness capabilities and that FEMA's indicator for determining whether to recommend that a jurisdiction receive disaster assistance does not accurately reflect the ability of state and local governments to respond to disasters.[16] Had FEMA adjusted its indicator to reflect changes in personal income and inflation, 44 percent and 25 percent fewer disaster declarations, respectively, would have met the threshold for public assistance during fiscal years 2004 through 2011. In September 2012, we recommended, among other things, that FEMA develop a methodology to more accurately assess a jurisdiction's capability to respond to and recover from a disaster without federal assistance. FEMA concurred with this recommendation.

Federal Government as Property Owner and Operator

The federal government owns and operates hundreds of thousands of buildings and facilities that a changing climate could affect. For example, in its 2010 Quadrennial Defense Review, the Department of Defense (DOD) recognized the risk to its facilities posed by climate change, noting that the department must assess potential impacts and adapt as required.[17] We plan to report later this year on DOD's management of climate change risks at over 500,000 defense facilities. In addition, the federal government manages about 650 million acres—nearly 30 percent of the land in the United States—for a variety of purposes, such as recreation, grazing, timber, and fish and wildlife. In 2007, we recommended that that the Secretaries of Agriculture, Commerce, and the Interior develop guidance for their resource managers that explains how they expect to address the effects of climate change, and the three departments generally agreed with this recommendation.[18] However, as we showed in our May 2013 report, resource managers still struggled to incorporate climate-related information into their day-to-day activities, despite the creation of strategic policy documents and high-level agency guidance.[19]

Federal Government As Provider of Technical Assistance to State and Local Governments

The federal government invests billions of dollars annually in infrastructure projects that state and local governments prioritize and supervise. In total, the United States has about 4 million miles of roads and 30,000 wastewater treatment and collection facilities. According to a 2010

Congressional Budget Office report, total public spending on transportation and water infrastructure exceeds $300 billion annually, with roughly 25 percent of this amount coming from the federal government and the rest coming from state and local governments.[20] These projects have large up-front capital investments and long lead times that require decisions about addressing climate change before its potential effects are discernable. The federal government plays a limited role in project-level planning for transportation and wastewater infrastructure, and state and local efforts to consider climate change in infrastructure planning have occurred primarily on a limited, ad hoc basis.

Infrastructure is typically designed to withstand and operate within historical climate patterns. However, according to NRC, as the climate changes and historical patterns—in particular, those related to extreme weather events—no longer provide reliable predictions of the future, infrastructure designs may underestimate the climate-related impacts to infrastructure over its design life, which can range as long as 50 to 100 years.[21] These impacts can increase the operating and maintenance costs of infrastructure or decrease its life span, or both, leading to social, economic, and environmental impacts.

For example, the National Oceanic and Atmospheric Administration estimates that, within 15 years, segments of Louisiana State Highway 1— the only road access to Port Fourchon, which services virtually all deep-sea oil operations in the Gulf of Mexico, or about 18 percent of the nation's oil supply—will be inundated by tides an average of 30 times annually due to relative sea level rise. Flooding of this road effectively closes this port. Because of Port Fourchon's significance to the oil industry at the national, state, and local levels, the U.S. Department of Homeland Security, in July 2011, estimated that a closure of 90 days could reduce the national gross domestic product by $7.8 billion.[22] Figure 1 shows Louisiana State Highway 1 leading to Port Fourchon.

Despite the risks posed by climate change, we found, in April 2013, that infrastructure decision makers have not systematically incorporated potential climate change impacts in planning for roads, bridges, and wastewater management systems because, among other factors, they face challenges identifying and obtaining available climate change information best suited for their projects.[23] Even where good scientific information is available, it may not be in the actionable, practical form needed for decision makers to use in planning and designing infrastructure. Such decision makers work with traditional engineering processes, which often require very specific and discrete information. Moreover, local decision makers—who, in this case, specialize in infrastructure planning, not climate science—need assistance from experts who can help them translate available climate change information into something that is locally relevant. In our site visits to a limited number of locations where decision makers overcame these challenges— including Louisiana State Highway 1—state and local officials emphasized the role that the federal government could play in helping to increase their resilience.[24]

Source: NOAA.

Figure 1. Louisiana State Highway 1 Leading to Port Fourchon.

Any effective adaptation strategy must recognize that state and local governments are on the front lines in both responding to immediate weather-related disasters and in preparing for the potential longer-term impacts associated with climate change. We reported, in October 2009, that insufficient site-specific data—such as local temperature and precipitation projections—complicate state and local decisions to justify the current costs of adaptation efforts for potentially less certain future benefits.[25] We recommended that the appropriate entities within the Executive Office of the President develop a strategic plan for adaptation that, among other things, identifies mechanisms to increase the capacity of federal, state, and local agencies to incorporate information about current and potential climate change impacts into government decision making. USGCRP's April 2012 strategic plan for climate change science recognizes this need by identifying enhanced information management and sharing as a key objective.

Our April 2013 report on infrastructure adaptation concluded that the federal government could help state and local efforts to increase their resilience by (1) improving access to and use of available climate-related information, (2) providing officials with improved access to local assistance, and (3) helping officials consider climate change in their planning processes.[26] In April 2013 we recommended, among other things, that the Executive Director of USGCRP or other federal entity designated by the Executive Office of the President work with relevant agencies to identify for decision makers the "best available" climate-related information for infrastructure planning and update this information over time, and to clarify sources of local assistance for incorporating climate-related information and analysis into infrastructure planning, and communicate how such assistance will be provided over time. They have not directly responded to these recommendations, but the President's June 2013 Climate Action Plan and November 2013 Executive Order 13653 on Preparing the United States for the Impacts of Climate Change drew attention to these issues.[27] For example, the Executive Order directs numerous federal agencies, supported by USGCRP, to work together to develop and provide authoritative, easily accessible, usable, and timely data, information, and decision-support tools on climate preparedness and resilience.

We also have work under way exploring, among other things, the risk extreme weather events and climate change pose to defense facilities, public health, agriculture, public transit systems, and federal insurance programs. This work—within the framework of the February 2013 high-risk designation—may identify other steps the federal government could take to limit its fiscal exposure and make our communities more resilient to extreme weather events.

Chairman Carper, Ranking Member Coburn, and Members of the Committee, this concludes my prepared statement. I would be pleased to answer any questions you have at this time.

End Notes

[1] Our past work identified a variety of fiscal exposures—responsibilities, programs, and activities that may either legally commit the federal government to future spending or create the expectation for future spending. Fiscal exposures vary widely as to source, extent of the government's legal commitment, and magnitude. Further, some of these factors may change

over time. For example, the government's response to an event or series of events can strengthen expectations that the government will respond in the same way to similar events in the future. For additional information, see Fiscal Exposures: Improving Cost Recognition in the Federal Budget, GAO-14-28 (Washington, D.C.: Oct. 29, 2013).

[2] Thomas R. Karl, Jerry M. Melillo, and Thomas C. Peterson, eds. Global Climate Change Impacts in the United States (Cambridge University Press: 2009). USGCRP coordinates and integrates the activities of 13 federal agencies that conduct research on changes in the global environment and their implications for society. USGCRP began as a presidential initiative in 1989 and was codified in the Global Change Research Act of 1990 [Pub. L. No. 101-606, § 103 (1990)]. USGCRP-participating agencies are the Departments of Agriculture, Commerce, Defense, Energy, Interior, Health and Human Services, State, and Transportation; U.S. Agency for International Development; Environmental Protection Agency; National Aeronautics and Space Administration; the National Science Foundation; and the Smithsonian Institution.

[3] The National Oceanic and Atmospheric Administration's National Climatic Data Center tracks and evaluates climate events in the United States and globally that have great economic and societal impacts.

[4] NRC, America's Climate Choices: Panel on Adapting to the Impacts of Climate Change, Adapting to the Impacts of Climate Change (Washington, D.C.: 2010). NRC is the principal operating agency of the National Academy of Sciences and the National Academy of Engineering.

[5] Congress temporarily increased the borrowing authority for the National Flood Insurance Program by $9.7 billion and provided about $50 billion in appropriated funds for expenses related to the consequences of Superstorm Sandy.

[6] GAO, High-Risk Series: An Update, GAO-13-283, February 2013. Every 2 years at the start of a new Congress, GAO calls attention to agencies and program areas that are high risk due to their vulnerabilities to fraud, waste, abuse, and mismanagement, or are most in need of transformation.

[7] FEMA has authority to borrow money from Treasury to pay losses that exceed premium revenue and any accumulated surplus. Treasury charges FEMA interest on the outstanding debt. Before Superstorm Sandy, this borrowing authority stood at $20.725 billion. In January 2013, Congress passed and the President signed into law a $9.7 billion increase in this authority to pay flood claims related to Superstorm Sandy, raising FEMA's borrowing authority to a total of $30.425 billion. Pub. L. No. 113-1, § 1(a), 127 Stat. 3, 3 (2013).

[8] GAO-14-28.

[9] GAO, Climate Change: Financial Risks to Federal and Private Insurers in Coming Decades Are Potentially Significant, GAO-07-285 (Washington, D.C.: Mar. 16, 2007).

[10] GAO, National Flood Insurance Program: Continued Attention Needed to Address Challenges, GAO-13-858T (Washington, D.C.: Sept. 18, 2013); GAO, Flood Insurance: Implications of Changing Coverage Limits and Expanding Coverage, GAO-13-568 (Washington, D.C.: July 3, 2013).

[11] GAO, FEMA: Action Needed to Improve Administration of the National Flood Insurance Program, GAO-11-297 (Washington, D.C.: June 9, 2011).

[12] Pub. L. No 112-141, Div. F, Tit. II, Subtit. A, § 100216(b), 126 Stat. 405, 927 (2012) (codified at 42 U.S.C. 4101b(b)).

[13] GAO, Flood Insurance: Strategies for Increasing Private Sector Involvement, GAO-14-127 (Washington, D.C.: Jan. 22, 2014).

[14] As reported by the Congressional Research Service in August 2013, Congress appropriates money to the Disaster Relief Fund to ensure that funding for disaster relief is available to help individuals and communities stricken by emergencies and major disasters. Congress also appropriates disaster funds to other accounts administered by other federal agencies pursuant to federal statutes that authorize specific types of disaster relief. The Disaster Relief Fund is generally funded at a level that is sufficient for what are known as "normal" disasters. These are incidents for which Disaster Relief Fund outlays are less than $500 million. When a large disaster occurs, additional funding for the Disaster Relief Fund may be provided through emergency supplemental appropriations. A supplemental appropriation generally provides additional budget authority during the current fiscal year to (1) finance activities not provided for in the regular appropriation or (2) provide funds when the regular appropriation is deemed insufficient. For more information, see Congressional Research Service, Disaster Relief Funding and Supplemental Appropriations for Disaster Relief, R40708, (Washington, D.C.: Aug. 5, 2013).

[15] GAO, Federal Disaster Assistance: Improved Criteria Needed to Assess a Jurisdiction's Capability to Respond and Recover on Its Own, GAO-12-838 (Washington, D.C.: Sept. 12, 2012).

[16] GAO, Managing Preparedness Grants and Assessing National Capabilities, GAO-12-526T (Washington, D.C.: Mar. 20, 2012). See also GAO, Disaster Response: Criteria for Developing and Validating Effective Response Plans, GAO-10-969T (Washington, D.C.: Sept. 22, 2010).

[17] The Quadrennial Defense Review is a legislatively mandated review of DOD strategies and priorities and is required to be conducted every 4 years.

[18] GAO, Climate Change: Agencies Should Develop Guidance for Addressing the Effects on Federal Land and Water Resources, GAO-07-863 (Washington, D.C.: Aug. 7, 2007).

[19] GAO, Climate Change: Various Adaptation Efforts Are Under Way at Key Natural Resource Management Agencies, GAO-13-253 (Washington, D.C.: May 31, 2013).

[20] Congressional Budget Office, Public Spending on Transportation and Water Infrastructure, Pub. No. 4088 (Washington, D.C.: November 2010).

[21] See, for example, NRC, Panel on Strategies and Methods for Climate-Related Decision Support, Committee on the Human Dimensions of Global Change, Informing Decisions in a Changing Climate (Washington, D.C.: 2009).

[22] Department of Homeland Security, National Infrastructure Simulation and Analysis Center, Risk Development and Modeling Branch, Homeland Infrastructure Threat and Risk Analysis Center, Office of Infrastructure Protection, In Collaboration with the National Incident Management Systems and Advanced Technologies Institute at the University of Louisiana at Lafayette, Louisiana Highway 1/Port Fourchon Study (July 15, 2011).

[23] GAO, Climate Change: Future Federal Adaptation Efforts Could Better Support Local Infrastructure Decision Makers, GAO-13-242 (Washington, D.C.: Apr. 12, 2013).

[24] To examine consideration of climate change in U.S. infrastructure planning, we visited a nonprobability sample of seven selected locations where decision makers had undertaken such planning—three locations focused on roads and bridges (Washington State Route 522; Interstate-10 Twin Span Bridge near New Orleans, Louisiana; and Louisiana State Highway 1) , two locations focused on wastewater management systems (King County Wastewater Treatment Division in Washington and the Milwaukee Metropolitan Sewerage District in Wisconsin), and two National Aeronautics and Space Administration centers (Johnson Space Center in Houston, Texas, and Langley Research Center in Hampton, Virginia).

[25] GAO, Climate Change Adaptation: Strategic Federal Planning Could Help Government Officials Make More Informed Decisions, GAO-10-113 (Washington, D.C.: Oct. 7, 2009).

[26] GAO-13-242.

[27] More information on the June 2013 Climate Action Plan and Executive Order 13653 can be found at http://www.whitehouse.gov/administration/eop/ceq/initiatives/resilience

INDEX

D

E

F

G

R

S

T

U

V

W